RAILROAD STATIONS IN THE GALLATIN AREA, MONTANA

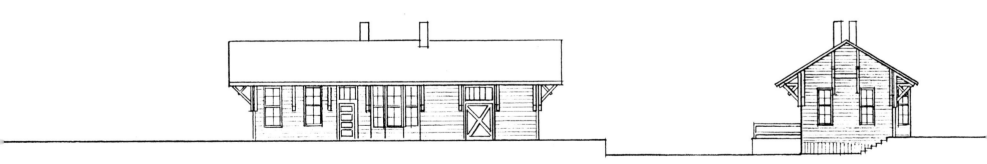

BY WILLIAM S. HOY

Cover Photo: Bozeman's first Northern Pacific depot served both passenger and freight traffic, just eight years, from 1883 to1891, when a larger passenger station was built a few blocks from the original site. The first building was used as a freight depot for a time. Note switch engines to the left of the depot; those tracks eventually became the Benepe and Ryan spurs.

Photo, Gallatin County Historical Society.

copyright 1998 by William S. Hoy

Keystone Press, P.O. Box 87152, Montgomery Village, MD 20886

ISBN 0-9668121-0-7

Library of Congress 98-75371

Printed by Artcraft Printers, Bozeman, Montana

sponsored by the

School of Architecture

Montana State University at Bozeman, Montana

and the

Gallatin County Historical Society

317 West Main Street, Bozeman, Montana

To members of my family who worked on the Pennsylvania Rail Road from 1850 through 1970: my grandfather James Hoy worked for the railroad; my great grandfather Michael Hoy completed fifty years of service with the Pensy; my great great grandfather also worked with the railroad; my great, great, great grandfather Barclay Hoy, helped lay the first Pensy tracks.

ACKNOWLEDGMENTS

During my visit to Montana in January 1998, I purchased *Bozeman and the Gallatin Valley* by Phyllis Smith. As I read the book, it brought back the energy and enthusiasm I had when I completed a research paper for an independent architectural history class at Montana State University in 1980.

My paper was entitled *Survey of Gallatin County Railroad Stations*. As I was compiling the research, veteran railroad man Warren McGee, Livingston, helped over and above what I requested of him. He offered the use of his photographs and gave me leads to others knowledgeable in the field. Thank you, Warren.

The late Merrill G. Burlingame, distinguished professor of history at Montana State University, also supplied photos and accounts of early railroad history. Kingston Heath, my professor in architectural history, also at Montana State University at the time, challenged me to observe the present and understand the past.

I am grateful to Phyllis Smith for accepting the challenge to edit and contribute to this work. Without her participation, I might have thought about completing the manuscript without actually doing it. Phyllis is a new friend and has provided her knowledge of the history of the Gallatin Valley to the research I completed in 1980. Both of us, I hope, have included an overall view of Gallatin County railroading since the day in 1883 when the first locomotive came chugging over the Bozeman Pass.

My wife and family have had to put up with my pursuit of various projects, for which I am grateful.

This book would never have been written were it not for the late song writer Frank Zappa, whose offering "Moving to Montana Soon...Gonna Be a Dental Floss Tycoon" encouraged me to attend Montana State University. I wasn't interested in dental equipment, but I had to find out about Montana.

I appreciate the sponsorship of the Gallatin County Historical Society; their generous action means a lot to me. And my thanks to Montana State University for providing me with a great educational foundation. The majority of the proceeds from the sale of this work will be donated to the School of Architecture, Montana State University, http://www.montana.edu/wwwarch.

Bill Hoy, Montgomery Village, Maryland, 1998

When families settled in the Gallatin Valley in the 1860s, they expected the arrival of a railroad at any time. They talked about it and planned for it. But a railroad car would not cross the county for another twenty years. When the trains finally did begin service in 1883, life changed for almost everyone.

No longer did farmers and merchants have to rely on freighting with wagons and mule trains. Nor did they have to wait weeks for seed or potato starts to come from Salt Lake City or Walla Walla in Washington Territory. Grain elevators were built near train stops as far north as Menard; stockyards became a standard fixture as far south as the stop at Anceney. Depots, some large, some small, some two-story, some elegant with brick or stone facing, dotted the landscape. A seat on the train was much more comfortable than being jostled about on a rattling stage coach.

Some of the earlier settlements had to move closer to the lines. Buildings in Old Town relocated in Three Forks; Moreland moved closer to what would become Manhattan. Gallatin City, however, gave up the ghost and died. Logan achieved unexpected prominence for a time because Northern Pacific officials decided it was the logical place to build branch lines to Helena and Butte.

Country folks could send butter, eggs, and vegetable produce to town on the Interurban and other local trains. Their children could commute to Bozeman to attend Gallatin County High School or Montana Agricultural College. Farm women could dress in their Sunday best and take the train to town for a day of shopping. Belgrade became a community because of the railroad.

Today, no passengers board trains in the Gallatin Valley. Farm produce arrives at market by truck. The Gallatin Gateway Inn is once again elegant but tourists no longer step down from their Pullman to enter the great hall. Some of the train depots of an earlier day, however, have left us with a distinctive architecture, a few in good shape, most crumbling and abandoned. Bill Hoy offers this volume to those who enjoy reading about railroad depots of an earlier era.

Phyllis Smith, Bozeman, Montana

The photographer climbed to the edge of the Story Hills with his panoramic camera to capture an early view of Bozeman, some time between 1908 and 1916. In the middle foreground is the Northern Pacific roundhouse, just beyond it is the Bozeman Depot. Looking south toward Lone Mountain and the Spanish Peaks in the Madison Range is the fledgling Montana Agricultural College. *Photo, Gallatin County Historical Society.*

Table of Contents

CHAPTER ONE

INTRODUCTION

When the Northern Pacific Railway's first train pulled into Bozeman on March 21, 1883, it was met by a large parade from the courthouse to the depot, even though some celebrants were deterred by muddy unpaved streets on the way to the station. [1]

The coming of the railroad attracted a greater variety of laboring groups, new merchants, more homesteaders, and a rising number of tourists. As the local economy broadened, additional building needs became evident. The purpose of this book is to discuss some of the developing needs to house goods and to render services required by the railroad and its customers: the construction of depots. Veteran railroad conductor Warren R. McGee says that some communities welcomed first trains with a boxcar for a depot. [2] Larger railroad companies, however, were ready with a variety of distinctive architectural designs for stations.

Railroad service was expected by Gallatin Valley residents as early as 1863, when first settlements were established in the western portion of the valley. Little did they realize that twenty years would pass before the first Northern Pacific locomotive would chug across Bozeman Pass into the Gallatin Valley. Surveys were completed by 1871, but the financial panic of 1873 back in the States caused Northern Pacific to stop construction at Bismarck in Dakota Territory. J. W. Cooke and Company, the financial arm of the railroad, fell apart. A healthier economy ten years later finally allowed construction to continue west. In

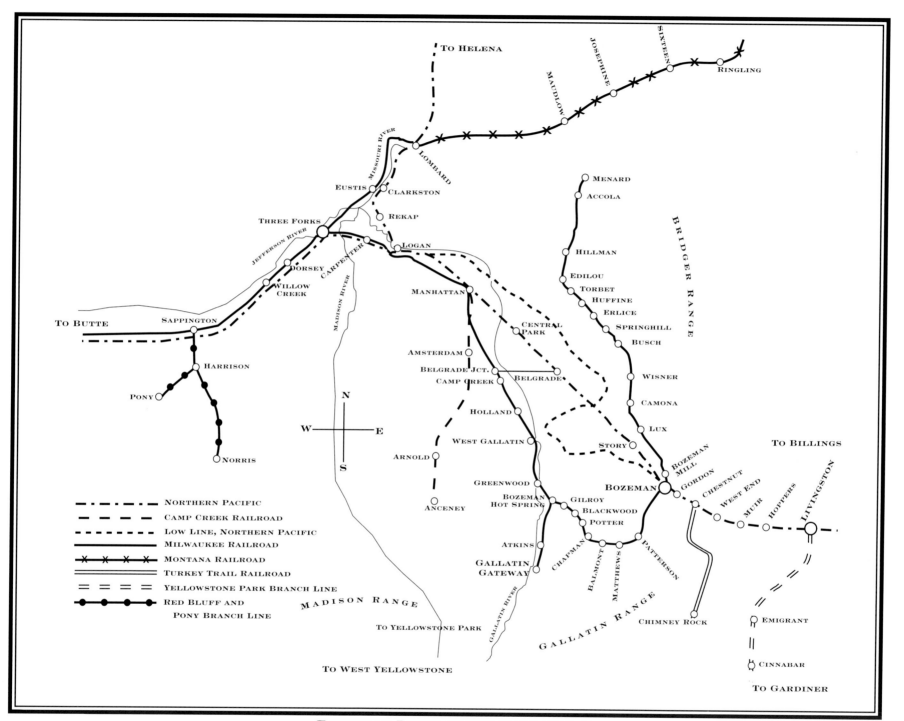

TO HELENA

JOSEPHINE

SIXTEEN

MAUDLOW

RINGLING

MISSOURI RIVER

LOMBARD

MENARD

ACCOLA

EUSTIS

CLARKSTON

REKAP

THREE FORKS

HILLMAN

BRIDGER RANGE

LOGAN

EDILOU

JEFFERSON RIVER

CARPENTER

TORBET

HUFFINE

DORSEY

ERLICE

WILLOW CREEK

MANHATTAN

SPRINGHILL

MADISON RIVER

TO BUTTE

SAPPINGTON

BUSCH

AMSTERDAM

CENTRAL PARK

WISNER

BELGRADE JCT.

HARRISON

CAMP CREEK

BELGRADE

CAMONA

PONY

LUX

HOLLAND

N

W   E

STORY

TO BILLINGS

S

WEST GALLATIN

NORRIS

BOZEMAN MILL

ARNOLD

GORDON

CHESTNUT

WEST END

MUIR

HOPPERS

LIVINGSTON

GREENWOOD

BOZEMAN

ANCENEY

BOZEMAN HOT SPRING

GILROY

NORTHERN PACIFIC

BLACKWOOD

POTTER

CAMP CREEK RAILROAD

LOW LINE, NORTHERN PACIFIC

ATKINS

MILWAUKEE RAILROAD

CHAPMAN

PATTERSON

MONTANA RAILROAD

GALLATIN GATEWAY

BALMONT

MATTHEWS

TURKEY TRAIL RAILROAD

GALLATIN RANGE

YELLOWSTONE PARK BRANCH LINE

RED BLUFF AND PONY BRANCH LINE

MADISON RANGE

GALLATIN RIVER

CHIMNEY ROCK

EMIGRANT

TO YELLOWSTONE PARK

CINNABAR

TO WEST YELLOWSTONE

TO GARDINER

RAILROAD LINES IN THE GALLATIN AREA

due time, the Northern Pacific also supported branch lines in the region, one through coal bearing country at the eastern end of the county, the Turkey Trail Railroad; another from Livingston south to Cinnabar, the Rocky Mountain Railroad of America, later called the Yellowstone Park Branch Line; one leading to cattle country at the boundary of the Flying D Ranch, at first called the Camp Creek Railway; and a low line freight route which ran through agricultural lands at a grade less steep than the main line.

A decade later, railroad entrepreneur Richard Harlow began construction of The Montana Railroad, a line that started in Lombard on the Missouri River, ran east through Sixteenmile Canyon to Ringling, east to Harlowton, with a terminus to the north at Lewistown. Harlow dreamed of freighting ore from the mining town of Castle to smelters at Helena. He talked so persuasively about his plans that the railroad came to be known as "The Jawbone." The line was completed in 1897; passengers traveling to the west and freight as well were transferred to the Northern Pacific trains waiting at Lombard.

In 1908, the Chicago, Milwaukee, St. Paul and Puget Sound Railway Company (later shortened to The Milwaukee Road) acquired The Jawbone line to provide another link to its transcontinental route. The Milwaukee Road owners continued construction from Lombard to Three Forks, and then westward. Thus, Gallatin County could boast of two transcontinental railroads. The Milwaukee Road also invested in Bozeman's streetcar line as well as an interurban running from town to Salesville (now called Gallatin Gateway). For a time, the Milwaukee Road supported a branch line, the Turkey Red Special, that ran north from Bozeman to the little town of Menard.

By 1912, the Gallatin Valley had well over two hundred miles of railroad track winding through its agricultural lands; located along that track were forty-eight railroad depots. Twenty-three of these belonged to the Northern Pacific, twenty-four were owned by the Milwaukee Road, and one large depot at

West Yellowstone was part of the Union Pacific holdings. From 1883 to 1998, Gallatin County has had a total of almost one hundred railroad station buildings and small lean-to structures. Some towns have had more than one depot. A good number of these buildings have moved or vanished or are used now for a different purpose.

A variety of power sources pushed the trains of these lines: water produced electricity to run Bozeman's streetcars, the interurban, and, later, the Milwaukee's electric line to Three Forks until 1932. Coal, much of it mined in the hills east of the Gallatin Valley, fed Northern Pacific locomotives until the introduction of diesel power in 1954. The Milwaukee Road discontinued its passenger service in 1963. Northern Pacific stopped taking reservations for passenger travel before May 1, 1971. For a time, Amtrak carried travelers, but it too discontinued service to the Gallatin Valley on October 2, 1979. By 1987, Burlington Northern had acquired the Northern Pacific holdings in Montana and those of the Milwaukee Road as well. Montana Rail Link, Inc., leased lines from Burlington Northern in 1987 and is presently a state freight carrier.

Passenger service is long gone from the Gallatin Valley, but at night, residents can wake to hear modern whistles as trains haul freight back and forth from Three Forks to the Bozeman Tunnel under Bozeman Pass.

CHAPTER TWO

NORTHERN PACIFIC RAILWAY THE MAIN LINE

As railroading building capital became more available in the early 1880s, the Northern Pacific

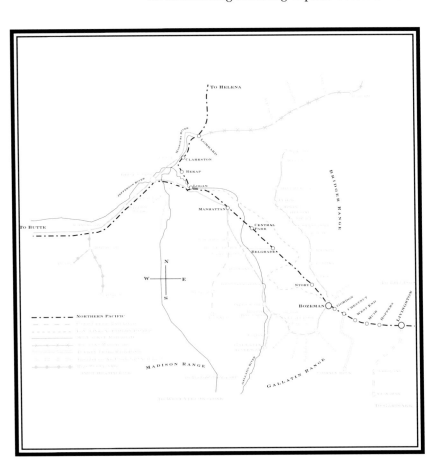

Railway lost no time in laying track west from Bismarck, Dakota Territory. When the line reached Livingston in 1882, company officials designated this Montana Division as District One, originating in Livingston and terminating at Helena. Hence, Livingston developed into a major center for railroad traffic as well as an important repair facility. In 1883, the trains were forced to travel over Bozeman Pass until Muir Tunnel was completed one year later. The tunnel was 3,610 feet long. Elevation at the tunnel was the highest at that time along the entire Northern Pacific line at 5,592 feet. (Later on, Homestake Pass would become the highest point.) From the train stop at Muir to the depot at Logan the terrain dropped 1,392 feet.

Left: Livingston's second Northern Pacific Depot, 1890. *Photo, Warren R. McGee.*

Right: Livingston Depot as viewed from the tracks, c1980. *William S. Hoy photo.*

Above: Exterior detail from the Livingston Depot, c1980. *William S. Hoy photo.*

Below: Trackside elevation drawing from the office of C. A. Reed and A. H. Stem, Associates, St. Paul, Minnesota.

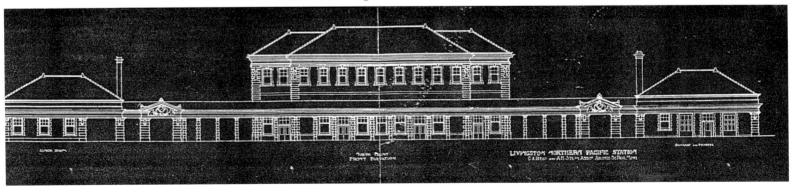

Left: The stop at Hoppers on the way west to the Muir Tunnel and Bozeman, 1920. *Photo, Warren R. McGee.*

Right: Nearing the eastern entrance to the Muir Tunnel. *Warren R. McGee photo.*

For most railroad stops, the Northern Pacific followed other major railroads of the nineteenth century and built standard depots from a "Systems Standards" manual, based on the existing or anticipated importance of the location. These included the:

1) Urban Form
2) Medium Rural Form
3) Standard Form

The majority of the Northern Pacific stations were developed in the main Office of the Engineer in St. Paul, Minnesota. Company architects paid attention to current styles and used easily obtainable materials that adapted well to particular shelters.

The Gallatin Valley has supported all three types during its one hundred and five-year railroad history. Bozeman's second and third (the second depot was revamped) stations exemplify the Urban Form, borrowing styles that were popular in the late l880s by architect H. H. Richardson and some of the rural

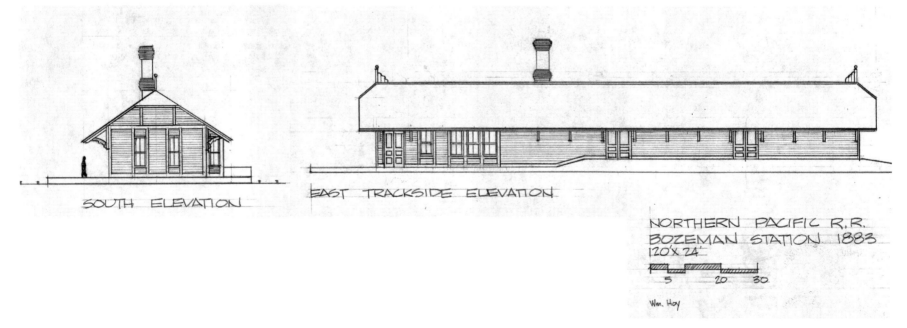

SOUTH ELEVATION

EAST TRACKSIDE ELEVATION

NORTHERN PACIFIC R.R.
BOZEMAN STATION 1883
120' x 24'

5   20   30

Wm. Hoy

stations of Frank Furness. In Gallatin County, Northern Pacific stations were designed by staff designers rather than by independent architects. Some depots in the surrounding area, however, were designed by prominent nineteenth century architects, i.e., the third station at Livingston (Reed and Stem), the depot at Gardiner (Robert Reamer), and the structure at Butte (Reed and Stem).

The depots at Logan and Trident express the Medium Rural Form by showing a limited amount of architectural styles of their period, i.e., Logan's small outcropping of windows on the roof and Trident's use of crenelation. Designers of both these stations were influenced by Richardson's attitudes toward railroad stations as places where passengers would feel secure during their travels. The depots were built low to the ground with, perhaps, a gable on a hip roof, suggesting a safe place for shelter and waiting.

Most of the Northern Pacific stations in the Gallatin Valley represent the Standard Form, a utilitarian design for transportation and trade. Both Bozeman's and Manhattan's first stations are good examples of simple functional structures — not showy but of honest design. Bozeman's first station illustrates the Standard Form by the use of materials and the representation style common to Northern Pacific rural stations, i.e., long vertical windows and standard milled knee braces. (See Appendix, pages 105-119 for Northern Pacific's standard station designs.) The main line and its depot were located away from the original platted city on sixteen acres of land donated by the McAdow Flour Mill. Local merchants priced their lots in town at too high a level to interest railroad officials. Although the depot was welcomed by local residents as a sign of

Bozeman's second Northern Pacific Depot in 1918 before renovation. *Photo, Warren R. McGee.*

civic progress, it soon became apparent that the little depot was inadequate to Bozeman's growing commercial prominence — either real or perceived. Eight years later, local businessmen wanted a new depot.

On July 4, 1891, the *Bozeman Avant Courier* took note of a visit by Northern Pacific executives "to select and designate the site for the long-talked-of and greatly needed passenger and freight depot, and to

Train passing remodeled Northern Pacific Depot, Bozeman, June 1, 1939. Note low line coal dock and water tank in distance. *Photo, Gallatin County Historical Society.*

ascertain what extensions and improvements are needed in the company's yards." The editor went on to state that some of the townspeople were unhappy with Northern Pacific's requirement that Bozeman raise some $6,000 for a $10,000 depot. But, he added philosophically, what could be done about it? We had better "put up or shut up." We need a new depot. "the little, dingy, cobby-hole of a passenger depot, containing neither a waiting room for ladies nor other usual and necessary accomodations [sic] for patrons of the road, is a standing disgrace, both to the city and to the railroad company..." The editor continued, "It wouldn't, perhaps, be the proper thing to encourage petty larceny, but under the circumstances, if some able-bodied, unfortunate tramp should come along during the dark of the moon and carry off bodily the Bozeman 'passenger depot' and trade it to some farmer, in need of a chicken coop," who would complain? [3]

BN DEPOT 1978
BOZEMAN, MONT.

Evidently, civic grumbling paid off; on November 28, 1891, the same newspaper reported, "The new depot is gradually assuming permanent

The Bozeman Depot in 1978, the year before Amtrak passenger service was discontinued.
Photo, Gallatin County Historical Society.

shape. It presents quite a neat and substantial appearance and will be an ornament to that part of the city." [4]
The Bozeman Weekly Chronicle, a new competitor to the *Avant Courier,* described the finished building to its readers one month later:

> The railroad depot just completed to fill the requirements of an increasing business is an architectural exotic. It is of brick, with stone trimmings, 30' X 92'. Gentlemen's waiting room, 20 X 28; ladies the same size. Five foot passage way between. Baggage room, 17' X 28', express office same. Finished throughout in hardwood and provided with fixtures for water, gas and electricity. It has a 700 foot platform. [5]

The newspaper also mentioned that the new depot was built for $15,000 but did not state how much of that sum was paid by Bozeman residents. This station is the oldest existing depot in the Gallatin Valley.

Waiting room of Northern Pacific Depot.
Dennis Seibel photo,
Gallatin County Historical Society.

Two views of Bozeman's
Northern Pacific Depot, 1980.
William Hoy photos.

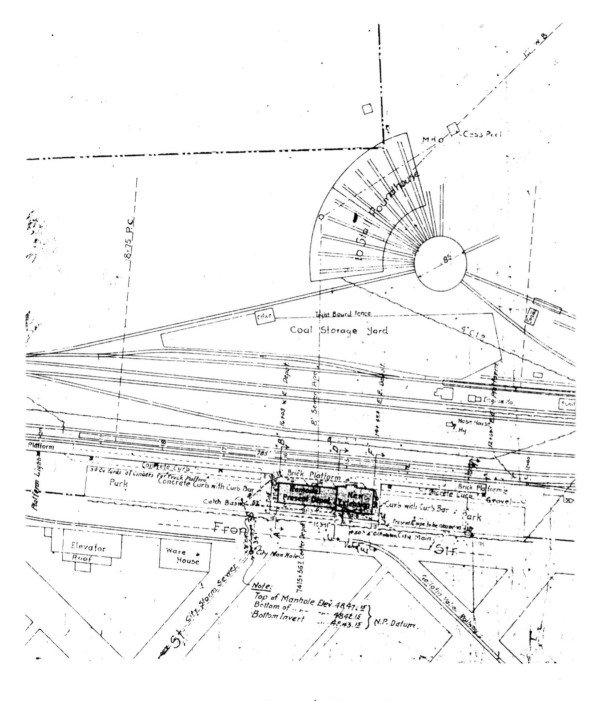

Bozeman's third station site plan

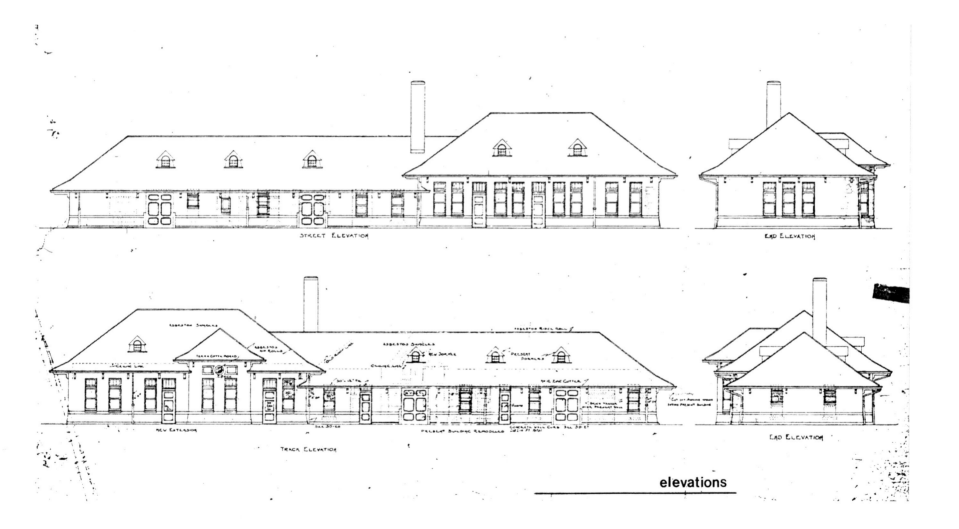

STREET ELEVATION

END ELEVATION

TRACK ELEVATION

END ELEVATION

elevations

16

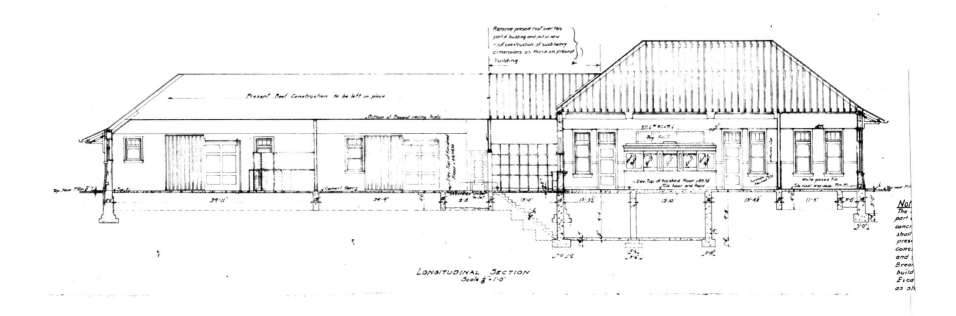

Remove present roof over this
part of building and put in new
roof construction of such heavy
dimensions as those on present
building.

Present Roof Construction to be left in place

Bottom of Present ceiling Joists

LONGITUDINAL SECTION
Scale ⅛" = 1'-0"

section

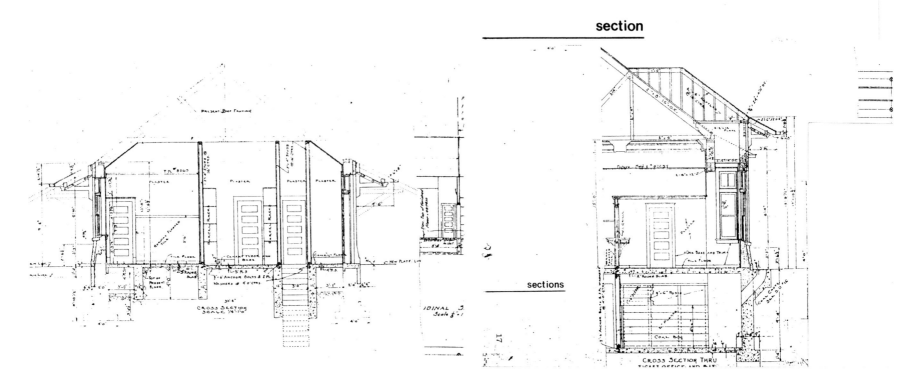

CROSS SECTION
Scale ¼" = 1'-0"

sections

CROSS SECTION THRU
TICKET OFFICE AND BAY

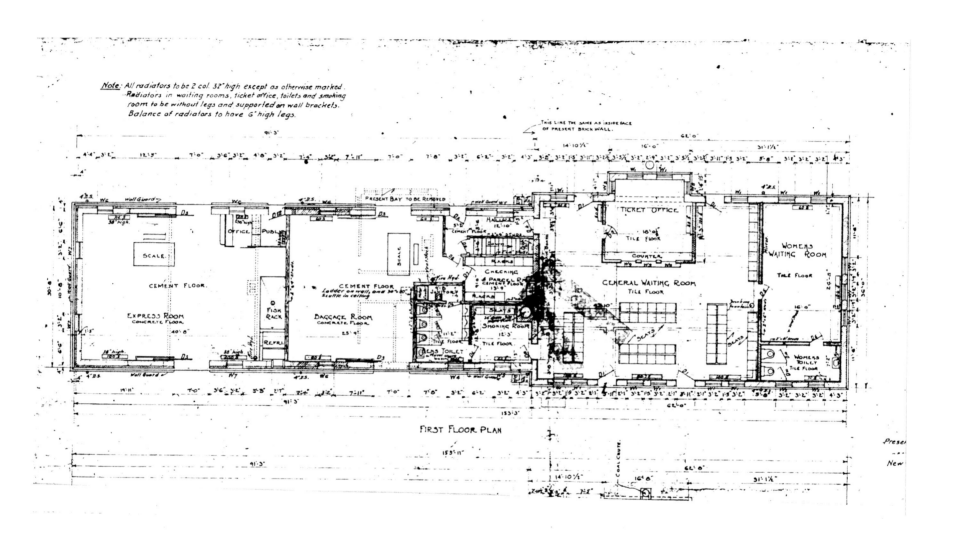

Note: All radiators to be 2 col. 32" high except as otherwise marked.
Radiators in waiting rooms, ticket office, toilets and smoking room to be without legs and supported on wall brackets.
Balance of radiators to have 6" high legs.

THIS LINE THE SAME AS INSIDE FACE OF PRESENT BRICK WALL.

PRESENT BAY TO BE REMOVED

EXPRESS ROOM
CONCRETE FLOOR.
CEMENT FLOOR.

BAGGAGE ROOM
CONCRETE FLOOR.
CEMENT FLOOR

OFFICE   PUBL.

FISH RACK

REFRI.

GENTS TOILET

SMOKING ROOM
TILE FLOOR

CHECKING & PARCELS R.
CEMENT FLOOR

HALL
CEMENT FLOOR

TICKET OFFICE
TILE FLOOR
COUNTER

GENERAL WAITING ROOM
TILE FLOOR

SEATS

WOMENS WAITING ROOM
TILE FLOOR

WOMENS TOILET
TILE FLOOR

FIRST FLOOR PLAN

COAL CHUTE

Presen

New

plan

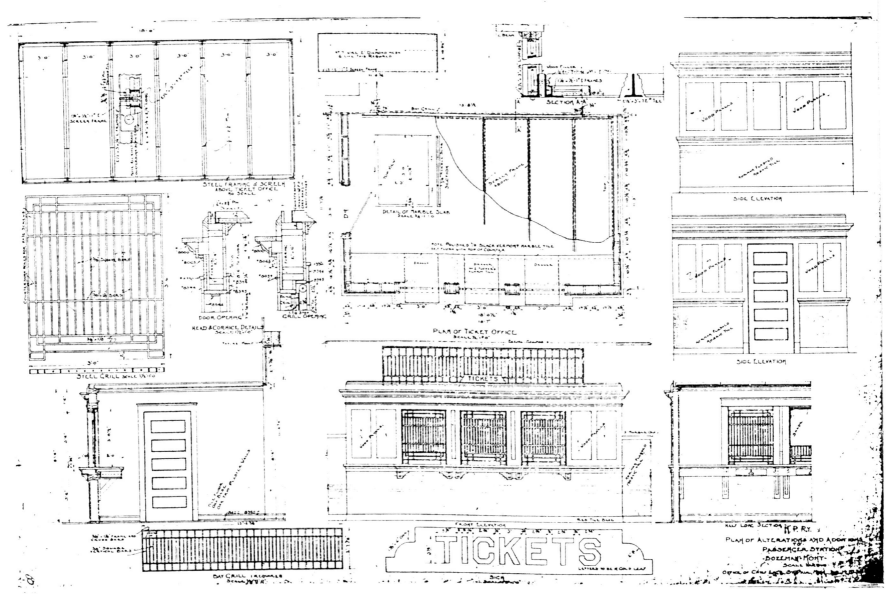

ticket office

Above: Northern Pacific's roundhouse at the northern edge of Bozeman, 1880s.

Right: Bozeman roundhouse in flames, late 1940s.

See page 117 for Standard Drawing.

Photos, Gallatin County Historical Society.

Last day of operation for steam switch engine #1093, April 9, 1955. Engineer: Cliff Garver. Conductor: Warren R. McGee.
Photo, Gallatin County Historical Society.

Four men pose with Northern Express delivery truck, 1917, 9 East Main Street. L-R: Rex LaBertew, Jesse Patrick (agent), Frank Sexton (driver), Dewey Pratt. *Photo, Gallatin County Historical Society.*

Belgrade's first Northern Pacific station was built in 1886 by contractor Alfred Lycan — a wood frame building designed in the Standard Form, measuring twenty by one hundred feet. The *Avant Courier* commented: "Contract let April 20, 1886 for erection of a large railway station, grain warehouse, and general store."[6] The structure burned down in the 1930s and was immediately replaced by the present depot, measuring twenty by sixty feet, a good example of a smooth surface building, reflecting the architectural trends of that day.

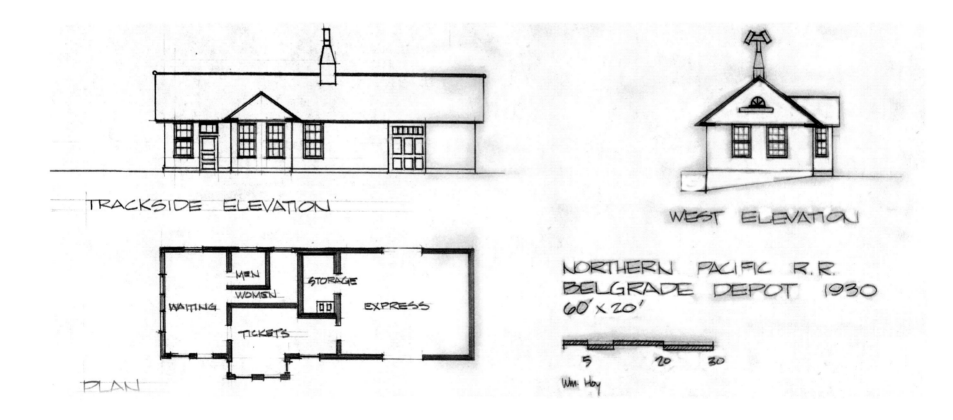

TRACKSIDE ELEVATION

WEST ELEVATION

PLAN

MEN
WOMEN
STORAGE
WAITING
EXPRESS
TICKETS

NORTHERN PACIFIC R.R.
BELGRADE DEPOT 1930
60' x 20'

5   20   30

Wm. Hoy

Left: Looking east at the Northern Pacific's Belgrade Depot, 1948. *Warren R. McGee photo.*

Above: Belgrade's second Northern Pacific Depot, 1980. *William Hoy photo.*

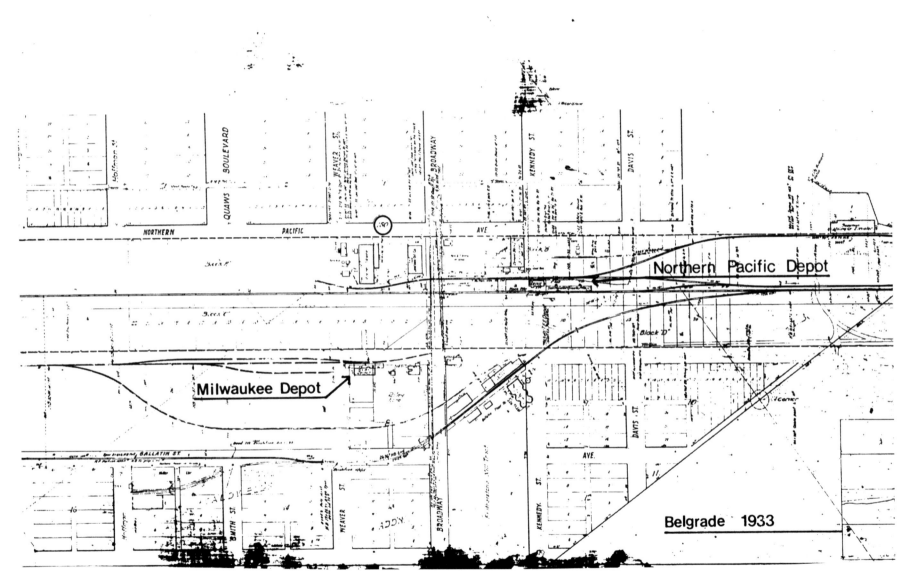

Plat showing Belgrade's depots, 1933.

To the west, the little village of Hamilton was moved closer to the Northern Pacific lines and renamed Moreland by British residents who had come to raise cattle and thoroughbred horses. Railroad officials built a depot at Moreland, soon to change its name again to Manhattan, reflecting the New York-based interests who started a malting industry at that location in 1891. Built in the typical Standard Form popular in the 1880s, this railroad station was the oldest remaining depot in the Gallatin Valley until it was moved to Emigrant in the mid 1980s and used as a museum for a time. Wood framed, this twenty by sixty foot structure was similar in appearance to Bozeman's first depot. It is dissected by a bay trackside window; inside are hardwood floors. The Manhattan Depot is a fine example of an early railroad station form built in a rural area.

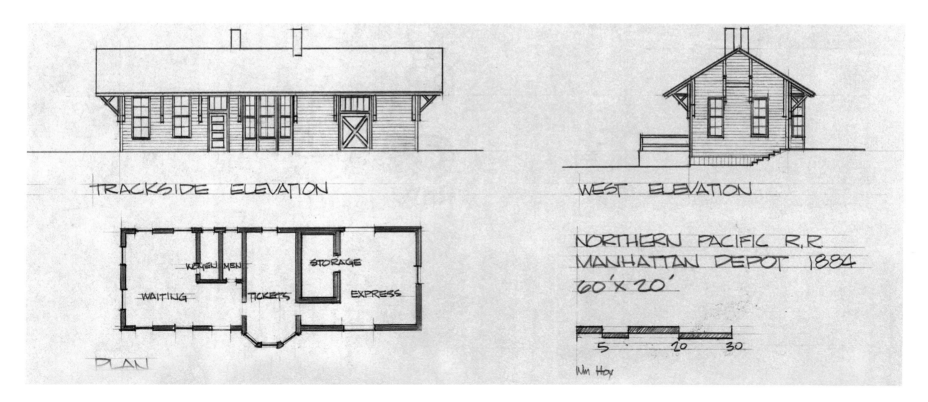

TRACKSIDE ELEVATION

PLAN

WOMEN MEN   STORAGE

WAITING   TICKETS   EXPRESS

WEST ELEVATION

NORTHERN PACIFIC R.R
MANHATTAN DEPOT 1884
60' X 20'

5   20   30

Wm Hoy

Below: The station at Manhattan stands alone, left background, in 1892. Building in foreground is part of the Manhattan Malting Company. *Photo, Gallatin County Historical Society.*

Right: Manhattan Depot, 1980, some time before its removal to Emigrant. *Photo, William S. Hoy.*

When the Northern Pacific competed its Butte Short Line in 1890, Logan became a major division point and maintained its importance on the line through the Gallatin Valley until the advent of diesel engines in 1954. The little town became the stopping point for all passenger trains because of its mid-valley location, an ideal transfer point either to Butte or to Helena. In 1890, Logan's first depot was located on the south side of the mainline, measuring 24 by 54 feet. It was probably constructed of wood, and reflected the rural station form common in the late 1880s.

Left: The once-elegant depot at Logan, 1918, combined a railroad station, freight room, waiting areas for both men and women, and a ticket office. Connected to the depot by a breezeway was a popular beanery. *Photo, Gallatin County Historical Society.*

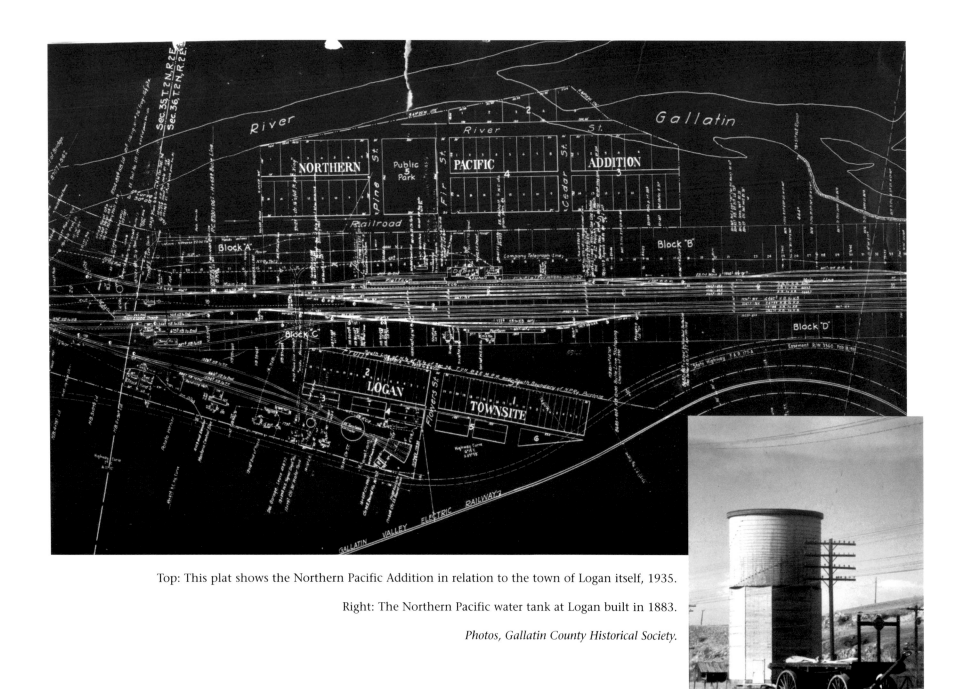

Top: This plat shows the Northern Pacific Addition in relation to the town of Logan itself, 1935.

Right: The Northern Pacific water tank at Logan built in 1883.

Photos, Gallatin County Historical Society.

With an increase in passenger travel, the Northern Pacific decided to construct a larger station complete with slate hip roof broken by outcrops and gable, and no indication of knee braces, giving the structure a low horizontal representation, an exterior that could be considered an example of Medium Rural Form. Its interior floors were marble; in the waiting room, tile lined the walls to a height of five feet. In addition to these elegant features, the Logan depot was also host to The Beanery, a restaurant open at all hours for the benefit of arriving passengers as well as residents from miles around who patronized the cafe regularly. The depot at Logan was torn down during the summer of 1971.

Since Gallatin City was situated near the confluence of three rivers — the Jefferson, the Madison, the Gallatin — officials of the Northern Pacific assumed that the village would become a prosperous town. They platted 320 lots of railroad land on a Gallatin City addition and built Gallatin Station, which the *Avant Courier* described as "a little frame structure close to the track [which] does serve as station house, ticket and telephone office." [7] Further exciting news in the newspaper:

What a disastrous 1919 fire at Logan did to railroad tracks.
Photo, Gallatin County Historical Society.

"Orders were received Monday at Gallatin to at once commence the construction of stock yards at that point. A depot building will also be put in...." [8] How long the depot at Gallatin Station survived is lost to history, as Gallatin City never flourished. Much of the wood from Gallatin City buildings was carried away by farmers and ranchers for use on their properties.

Approximately two miles north of Gallatin Station was a cement manufacturing plant of sufficient size to merit a depot. The Trident station, which was designed in December 1910, is another excellent example, like Logan, of Medium Rural Form, common in Northern Pacific depots. The introduction of crenelation at each corner of the structure and the choice of materials emphasize a fortified impression relating to the Trident surroundings. It would seem that the Northern Pacific architects were intentional in their use of stylistic characteristics to complement the area.

The arid land surrounding the Trident Depot is spare, perhaps suggesting the design of the station.
Photo, Gallatin County Historical Society.

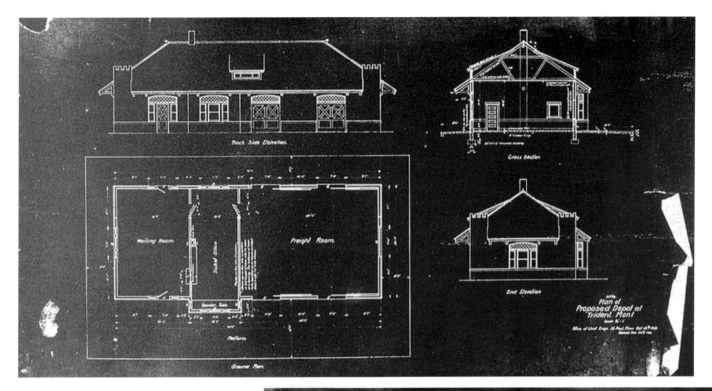

Renderings of Trident Depot.

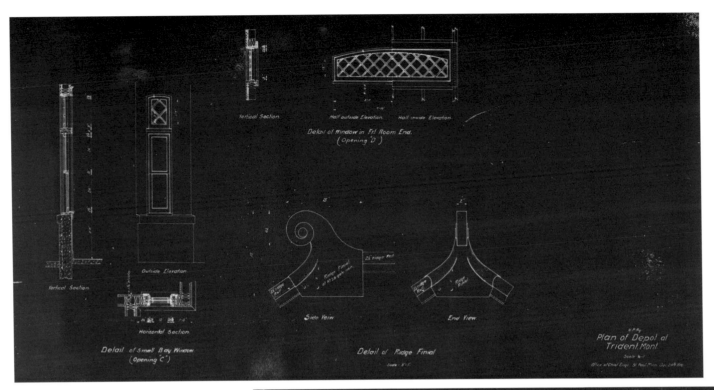

Renderings of Trident Depot.

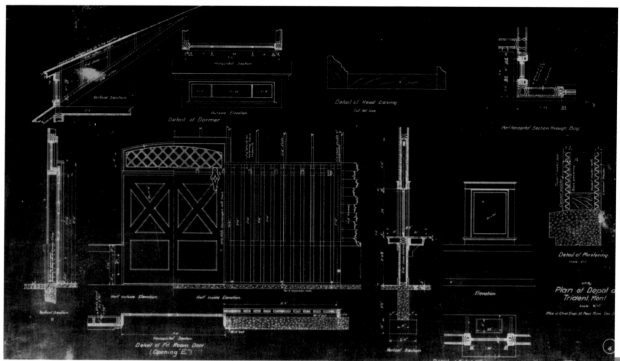

Rendering of Trident Depot.

Finished Trident Depot displays a fortress-like appearance with crenelation at each corner of the structure, c1980. *William S Hoy photo.*

An unusual shot: The Northern Pacific #1725 switches at Lombard's Milwaukee Road depot, 1950s. *Dorothy Nile photo, Gallatin County Historical Society.*

Proceeding northward, the depots at Clarkston and at Rekap were probably wooden structures in the Northern Pacific Standard Form. At the railhead of the Montana Railroad on the Missouri River near the town of Lombard, the Northern Pacific constructed a depot large enough to receive passengers and freight to and from the Montana Railroad (later acquired by the Milwaukee Road). The Lombard Depot was built in the Standard Form, a stripped down version of Bozeman's original station, big enough, however, to serve the transfer needs of the area.

Above: Two bridges crossed the Madison River east of Three Forks in 1918: The covered bridge was owned by the Milwaukee Road and the open steel bridge was on the Northern Pacific's Butte branch line. *Photo, Warren R. McGee.*

Left: Two electricfied trains pass one another near Willow Creek, November, 1928. *Photo, Gallatin County Historical Society.*

The Rural Form certainly described the Northern Pacific depots at Three Forks, Willow Creek, and Sappington. All had the same characteristics; no regional characteristics were incorporated into their design.

Northern Pacific depots in the Gallatin Valley exhibited all three styles. The company's designers adapted their Standard plans to fit this area with style and sensitivity, allowing extra funds to be spent on prominent locations of depots such as Bozeman and Logan.

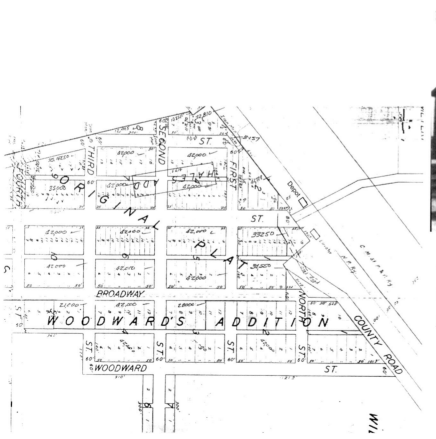

Above: A modest depot at Willow Creek.

Left: An early plat for Willow Creek.

Photos, Gallatin County Historical Society.

The Northern Pacific's low line, built in 1918, carried east-bound freight — no passengers. The route was constructed because of the difficulties encountered by steam locomotives attempting to carry freight on the existing main line grade of one percent.

The low line grade was less severe at 0.4 percent and allowed the Northern Pacific to add more freight cars to each train, thus improving efficiency. To accomplish this shallower grade, the low line had to be, by necessity, nine miles longer than the high line (main line). It meandered through the Gallatin Valley from the high line at Logan to Bozeman where it again joined the main line.

As the Northern Pacific switched to diesel engines beginning in 1955, the low line became obsolete and discontinued operations at the end of 1956. Some remnants of the low line can still be seen north of Manhattan and Belgrade and west of Bozeman.

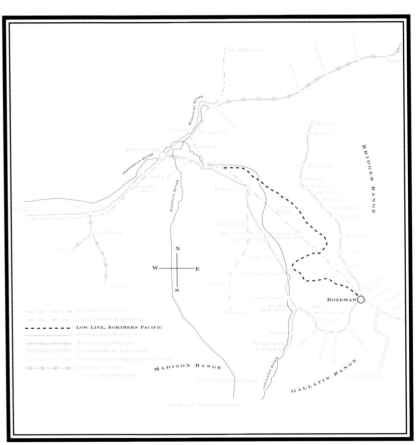

View of low line under construction from train on high line,
looking east, 1918.
Photo, Gallatin County Historical Society.

Looking west where the low line meets the high line, 1918.
Photo, Warren R. McGee.

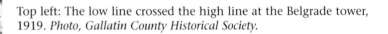

Top left: The low line crossed the high line at the Belgrade tower, 1919. *Photo, Gallatin County Historical Society.*

Above: The coal dock and water tank to serve the low line is under construction, April 1918; the tracks are not in place yet. *Photo, Gallatin County Historical Society.*

Left: The low line as it reached Bozeman at North Seventh Avenue, 1919. *Photo, Gallatin County Historical Society.*

Northern Pacific engine #5102 pulls freight on the low line. *Photo, Gallatin County Historical Society.*

The Northern Pacific leased two branch lines to pick up coal supplies for use in its own locomotives and to transport coke to the smelters at Anaconda, Butte, and East Helena. The first line, built in 1883, called officially the Rocky Mountain Railroad of America, ran from Livingston south to Brisbin, Trail Creek, Chicory, Emigrant, Daileys, Sphinx, and Horr, terminating at Cinnabar, a distance of fifty-one miles. The railroad freighted coal to larger cars waiting on the main line at Livingston.

Even before the Northern Pacific main line reached Livingston in 1882, however, officials in St. Paul had plans to use the coal branch line for a more lucrative purpose and it took a mere three years to

construct the line to Cinnabar. Ten years before, the U.S. Congress had designated the area south of Livingston as Yellowstone National Park. Everyone called it "Wonderland" and the Northern Pacific adopted the title as its own. Wonderland headlined their promotional posters and pamphlets. Each year, starting in 1895, the Northern Pacific issued the pamphlet *Wonderland*, written by Olin D. Wheeler, which featured articles about geysers and other thermal attractions. Some years, *Wonderland* discussed other parts of the the Northern Pacific route, or

Waiting for train to Gardiner and the north entrance of Yellowstone National Park, Livingston, 1910. *Photo, Warren R. McGee.*

the origin of its logo, but the magazine always had as its centerpiece news of Yellowstone National Park.

The depots at Livingston reflected the Northern Pacific's desire to attract affluent tourists. The 1890 station, by no means modest in character, was replaced in 1901-1902 by an even grander $75,000 structure. Designed by Reed and Stem, the architectural firm that designed New York's Grand Central Terminal and Tacoma's Union Station, the building was lined with distinctive Italian-style colonnades.

The tourist season began in mid-June and ended in mid-September. At first, stagecoaches met the travelers at Cinnabar and carried them seven miles into Gardiner. With the prospect of growing tourist dollars in mind, the Northern Pacific extended the line from Cinnabar to Gardiner in 1902, completing the work in 1904. The depot at Gardiner, designed by Seattle architect Robert Reamer, who also designed the Old Faithful Inn, featured a long curving loop. Editor Wheeler describes the resulting depot as:

> one of the most unique, cozy and attractive to be found in the United States. From the Bitterroot Valley and mountains, selected pine logs were brought which, with the smooth, richly colored bark on, were fashioned into a symmetric, well-proportioned, tasteful and rustic building, the interior of which, with its quaint hardware, comfortable, alluring appointments, and ample fireplace and chimney, is in keeping with the inviting exterior.

> Two colonnades, supported by massive, single log pillars at intervals, under which young and growing pine trees in wooden boxes are found, add much to the beauty of the structure. [9]

Wheeler continues to describe a pretty lake beside the station and to rhapsodize the mountain views beyond. "Back of the lake rises the high, brown-black lava arch and its side walls, the new and striking official entrance to Yellowstone park, costing $10,000, whose cornerstone President Roosevelt laid in 1903." [10]

President Theodore Roosevelt dedicated this arch near the north entrance to Yellowstone National Park in 1903. *Haynes photo, Gallatin County Historical Society.*

Both the Gardiner Depot and the arch can be seen in this broad photo. *Photo, Gallatin County Historical Society.*

It was not enough, however, to lure wealthy tourists to Wonderland. These visitors needed to be housed and fed during their park stay, in a manner commensurate with the richness of their pocketbooks. The railroad loaned money to concessioners who built such hostelries as the National Hotel in Mammoth Hot Springs in 1883, the Lake Hotel, and the Old Faithful Inn in 1904. These ventures catered to the rich. Round trip fare from St. Paul to Gardiner was forty-five dollars in 1905, out of reach for those of modest income. Fare from Livingston to Gardiner was five dollars, an expensive item when meals were added for an outrageous seventy-five cents apiece. After a leisurely ride on the Northern Pacific's Pullman Palace Car, the tourists were met at Gardiner by a stagecoach or tally-ho, capable of carrying thirty-seven passengers, pulled by six matched horses. On they went to the National Hotel where, after a day of sightseeing, they returned to change to formal attire for sumptuous evening dining and socializing with others of their financial rank. The Northern Pacific had no competition for tourist dollars until 1907, when the Union Pacific extended their line to the west entrance of the park. (See Chapter Five.)

In 1916, as stage coaches were being retired in favor of motorized touring vehicles, the railroad

The once-elegant station at Gardiner.
Photo, Warren R. McGee.

stepped in again to help fund the venture. During the 1920s, Northern Pacific added a more luxurious train, the *Yellowstone Comet*, which operated during the summer months only, outfitted with fancier cars and better accommodations. The Yellowstone Park Line was profitable until World War II, when the automobile supplanted the train, and personal visits to the park were available to those of more modest means and not restricted to group travel of the affluent. The distinctive curved depot at Gardiner was torn down in 1954. The tracks of the Yellowstone Branch Line were taken up in 1976. The original purpose of the branch line, the transportation of coal and coke to markets, decreased when such supplies could be obtained more cheaply elsewhere. It was not long before the coke ovens stopped production altogether.

The tracks pass Muir and west to the entrance of the new Bozeman Tunnel, finished in the summer of 1945. *Photo, Gallatin County Historical Society.*

TURKEY TRAIL RAILROAD

The second Northern Pacific branch line in this area was 11.2 miles of track, called the Turkey Trail Railroad, constructed in 1898, some of it with four and five percent grades. The line was operated by only the hardiest of railroad employees. It was a "top pay mountain railroad job for enginemen and trainsmen." [11] The grade presented special problems and mishaps were many. The Turkey Trail called at a number of coal mines in the region, running southeast from the main line at Chestnut to Storrs, Coulston, Hoffman, Kountz, Maxey, and Summit, ending at Chimney Rock. For a time, a modest narrow gauge line ran to the mines at Timberline as well.

Production was always limited in the Bozeman-Livingston Coal Field; although the product was of a fairly good quality, it was difficult to mine due to limestone fractures. When the smelter owners at Anaconda found a cheaper method to process their ores, and when coal from Utah became easier to procure, the small fields east of the Gallatin Valley closed down, one by one. Northern Pacific dropped its lease in 1914. The new owners hoped to attract the Milwaukee Road to acquire the line and continue it to the park's north boundary. They emphasized the line's other name, "Yellowstone Park Railway," but to no avail. The Turkey Trail Railroad stopped its operations in 1918 and the rails were shipped to France.

Timberline residents perch all about the little Heppie locomotive that pulled coal cars on the Turkey Trail.
Photo, Gallatin County Historical Society.

Looking over the Turkey Trail Railroad, 1915.
Photo, Warren R. McGee.

Below: Tracks lead into the Mountain Side mine, 1904. *Photo, Warren R. McGee*

Left: Company houses at the mining town of Storrs.
Photos, Warren R. McGee.

Right: The little depot at Chestnut, 1918, where
Northern Pacific leased a branch line into coal country.
Photos, Warren R. McGee.

CAMP CREEK RAILWAY COMPANY

Local Gallatin Valley interests built a modest fifteen-mile railway west of Bozeman from
Manhattan south to Anceney in 1911 to load cattle to market from the Flying D Ranch, one of the area's
largest ranches. The cars started to ship stock the following year. Two years later, the Northern Pacific
acquired the branch line and continued to ship cattle for a number of years. The tracks were used
occasionally until 1985, when the line was
abandoned.

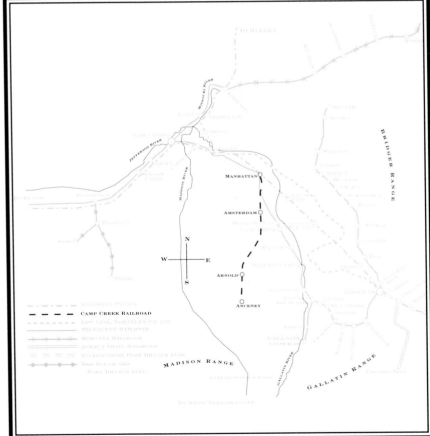

RED BLUFF AND PONY BRANCHES

In 1890, the Northern Pacific built the twenty-one-mile Red Bluff Branch line from Sappington to Norris to deliver mining equipment to nearby mining districts and to carry out gold ore to smelters. The once-thriving town of Red Bluff, located northeast of Norris, was a source of gold ore shipments. Another branch to Pony served the Mineral Hill mining district to bring in mining equipment to such mines as the Strawberry and carry out gold ore, bricks, and lumber. Sappington had livestock holding pens for cattle waiting for railroad transport to market. The lines were abandoned by the Northern Pacific in the early 1940s.

Mining equipment is delivered to Norris.
Photo, Gallatin County Historical Society.

Above: The Harrison station was moved to Virginia City in 1964 where it is part of a tourist attraction with a new sign, "Virginia City."

Left: Exterior detail from the Harrison Northern Pacific station, c1980. It is an excellent example of a combination depot second class as shown on page 113.

William S. Hoy photos.

Winter makes the Norris Northern Pacific station look even more desolate, c1980. For a time, the Norris Depot was home to the late newscaster Chet Huntley, whose father was a Northern Pacific telegrapher; the family lived at the back of the station.[12] The depot was moved twice: once for use as a Norris tire shop, then to a field on the road to Virginia City, three and one-half miles from Ennis. The once-elegant depot is now used for storage. Similar to First Class Standard Plan as shown on page 108. *William S. Hoy photo.*

NORTHERN PACIFIC RAILROAD.

MONTANA DIVISION

AND BRANCHES.

| No. 25 | TIME SCHEDULE | No. 25 |

TO TAKE EFFECT AT 11:59 P. M.

(MOUNTAIN OR 105th MERIDIAN TIME.)

(One hour slower than Central or 90th Meridian Time.)

SUNDAY, JUNE 4th, 1893.

SUCCEEDING CARDS AS SHOWN WITHIN.

For the government of employes only. The Company reserves the right to vary therefrom at pleasure. Be positive that you have the current card, and destroy all previous numbers. Read carefully the Special Rules, and always have for reference a copy of the TRANSPORTATION RULES.

M. C. KIMBERLY,   W. S. MELLEN,   G. W. DICKINSON,

BUTTE FREIGHT No. 59 Third Class DAILY	WAY FREIGHT No. 57 Third Class DAILY	FREIGHT No. 55 Third Class DAILY	EXPRESS FR'T No. 53 Second Class DAILY	Water, Coal, Scales, Tables and Wyes	Station Numbers	STATIONS	Distance from Livingston	PACIFIC MAIL No. 1 First Class DAILY	PACIFIC EX. VIA BUTTE No. 3 First Class DAILY	PACIFIC EX. VIA HELENA No. 5 First Class DAILY	BUTTE PASS. Pacific Mail Connection No. 7 First Class DAILY
De 9.00 P M M 56	De 5.00 A M	De 11.15 A M	De 7.45 P M	WCTSY	1071	Livingston 4.6	0.0	De 5.25 P M M 58	De 9.10 A M		
9.30 M 60	5.25	11.40 A M	8.10 M 56		1076	Coal Spur 4.4	4.6	* 5.35	F 9.20		
10.00	5.50	12.05 P M	8.35	W	1080	Hoppers 3.1	9.0	* 5.48	F 9.33		
10.20	6.10	12.25	8.50 M 60		1083	Muir 1.2	12.1	* 6.00 M 4	F 9.45		
10.30	6.20	12.35	9.00		1084	West End 0.6	13.3	* 6.06	F 9.51		
10.35	6.30	12.40	9.04		1085	Timber Line 1.9	13.9	* 6.08	F 9.53		
10.45	6.40	12.50	9.15		1087	Mountain Side 1.2	15.8	* 6.14	F 9.59		
10.50	6.50	12.56	9.20		1088	Chestnut 3.1	17.0	* 6.17	F 10.02		
11.05	7.05	1.12	9.35		1092	Gordon 4.7	20.1	* 6.24 M 56	F 10.09		
Ar 11.30 De 11.40 P M M 54	Ar 7.30 De 8.00	Ar 1.35 M 58 De 1.45 M 8	Ar 9.55 De 10.00	WCST	1096	Bozeman 4.6	24.8	Ar 6.35 De 6.40	Ar 10.20 De 10.25	De 10.40 A M	De 6.55 P M
12.01 A M	8.30	2.10	10.23		1101	Storey 5.1	29.4	* 6.48 M 60	F 10.35	F 10.50	F 7.03 M 60
12.21	9.00	2.35	10.45 M 54		1106	Belgrade 5.5	34.5	* 6.57	F 10.46	F 11.01	F 7.12
12.45	9.25	3.00	11.10	W	1111	Central Park 3.9	40.0	* 7.07	F 10.57	F 11.12	F 7.22
1.02	9.45	3.20 M 56	11.25		1115	Manhattan 5.4	43.9	* 7.15	F 11.05	F 11.20	F 7.30
Ar 1.25 AM M 2 DAILY See Page 5	10.15	Ar 3.45 De 3.50 M 6 & 4	11.45 P M	WC	1120	Logan 4.0	49.3	7.25	Ar 11.15 A M M 58 DAILY See Page 5	11.30 M 58	Ar 7.40 P M DAILY See Page 5
	10.35 M 58	4.05	12.05 A M	Y	1125	Gallatin 10.2	53.3	* 7.33		F 11.40	
	11.20	4.45	Ar 12.55 De 1.00 M 2		1135	Magpie 7.4	63.5	* 7.53		F 11.59 A M	
	11.50 A M	5.14	1.27	W	1142	Painted Rock 7.9	70.9	* 8.08 M 54		F 12.15 P M	
	Ar 12.27 P M 5 P De 12.37 M 56	5.45	1.55		1150	Toston 10.9	78.8	* 8.25		F 12.32 M 56 P 57	
	1.30	Ar 6.30 De 6.35 M 54	2.35	WCY	1161	Townsend 3.1	89.7	F 8.45		12.55	
H. B. V & B. and H. & J. C. FREIGHT No. 61 Third Class DAILY	Ar 1.55 De 2.00 M 6	6.50	2.50		1164	Bedford 5.4	92.8	* 8.53		F 1.03	
	2.25	7.15	3.15		1170	Vose 5.0	98.2	* 9.09		F 1.15	
	2.45	7.35	3.35		1175	Winston 8.8	103.2	* 9.22		F 1.25 M 6	
	3.25	8.20	4.10		1183	Clasoil 6.6	112.0	* 9.38		F 1.43	HELENA ACCN. No. 9 Second Class DAILY
De 4.35 P M M 54	Ar 4.30 M 54 9 P De 5.05	9.00	4.35	SY	1189	Prickley Pear Junc. 4.5	118.6	9.50		1.55	De 5.00 P M P 57 See 54
Ar 4.55 P M	Ar 5.25 P M	Ar 9.30 P M	Ar 5.00 A M M 58	WCSTY	1194	Helena	123.1	Ar 10.00 P M		Ar 2.05 P M	Ar 5.15 P M
DAILY	DAILY	DAILY	DAILY					DAILY		DAILY	DAILY

M—Meet.   P—Pass.   *—Trains do not stop for passengers.   F—Flag Station.   W—Water.   C—Coal.   S—Scale.   T—Table.   Y—Wye.

Study Carefully Special and General Rules.   Important changes have been made which must be understood alike by all.

Conductors will register at Livingston, Bozeman, Logan, Prickly Pear Junc. and Helena, and must not pass any registering station, which has telegraph service, without an order or clearance

Trains must be under perfect control when approaching switches and also all bluffs where slides are liable to occur.

When handling air-brake cars, descending mountain grades, the retaining valves must be applied. Conductors will be held responsible for this duty as well as releasing valves at foot of grades.

All Trains and Engines will reduce speed to five (5) miles per hour while passing through Bozeman Tunnel.

Built 1883

9-16-1883

FREIGHT No. 105 Third Class TUE., THUR. & SAT.	PASSENGER No. 103 First Class DAILY	Water, Coal, Scales, Tables and Wyes	Station Numbers	Distance from Livingston	Time Card No. 25 June 4th, 1893 Succeeding No. 24 A STATIONS	Distance from Cinnabar	Capacity of Side Tracks	Telegraph Offices	PASSENGER No. 104 First Class DAILY	FREIGHT No. 106 Third Class TUE., THUR. & SAT.
De 7.10 A M	De 9.15 A M	WCSTY	1071	0.0	Livingston 10.1	51.2	518	N	Ar 5.10 P.M	Ar 6.10 P M
7.50	F 9.32		TB10	10.1	Brisbin 4.4	41.1	6	F	4.53	5.25
8.07	F 9.38		TB14	14.5	Trail Creek 5.8	36.7	3	F	4.47	5.05
8.28	F 9.48	W	TB20	20.3	Chicory 2.9	30.9	24	F	4.37 P 106	De 4.42 / Ar 4.32 104 P
8.40	F 9.53		TB23	23.2	Emigrant 7.5	28.0	1	F	4.32	4.15
9.10	F 10.10		TB31	30.7	Daileys 9.8	20.5	12	F	4.15	3.45
9.50	F 10.37	W	TB41	40.5	Sphinx 9.2	10.7	12	F	3.48	3.00
10.50	11.05		TB49	49.7	Horr 1.5	1.5	25		3.20	2.00
Ar 11.05 A M See 103	Ar 11.10 A M	WY	TB51	51.2	Cinnabar	0.0	50	D	De 3.15 P M	De 12.30 P M
TUE., THUR. & SAT.	DAILY								DAILY	TUE., THUR. & SAT.

F—Flag Station.   W—Water.   C—Coal.   S—Scale.   T—Table.   Y—Wye.   D—Day and N—Night and Day Telegraph Office.

Fullfaced figures (1, 2, 3, etc.,) denote meeting and passing stations.

☞Study carefully Special and General Rules. Important changes have been made which must be understood alike by all.

Conductors will register at Livingston and Cinnabar, and must not pass any registering station, which has telegraph service, without an order or clearance.

Trains must not exceed Schedule Time without special orders, and **must be under perfect control** when approaching switches, also all bluffs where slides are liable to occur.

The switch at Livingston will be kept locked for N. P. main track. Conductors and engineers must protect their trains against all trains of Northern Pacific Railroad.

Passengers are allowed to ride only on rear section of regular trains.

All car doors must be kept closed while in trains.

No. 105 has right of track against 106, and No. 103 against No. 104, Livingston to Cinnabar.

J. D. FINN, Superintendent, Livingston.

Built 1890

7-10-90

7-10-90

7-10-90

MIXED No. 113 Second Class MON. WED. & FRI.	MIXED No. 109 Second Class MON. WED. & FRI.	Water, Coal, Tables and Wyes	Station Numbers	Distance	Time Card No. 25 June 4th, 1893 Succeeding No. 24 A STATIONS	Distance	Capacity of Side Tracks	Telegraph Offices	MIXED No. 110 Second Class MON. WED. & FRI.	MIXED No. 114 Second Class MON. WED. & FRI.
	See Page 5 / Ar 4.05 P M	WCY	TD 19	0.0	Sappington 9.5	20.6	60	D	De 11.55 A M	
	De 3.25 / Ar 2.25	Y	TE 9	9.5	Harrison 11.1	11.1	64		12.35 P M	
	De 1.40 P M	Y	TE 20	20.6	Norris	0.0	62	D	Ar 1.20 P M	
Ar 3.25 P M		Y	TE 9	0.0	Harrison 6.3	6.3	64			De 2.25 P M
De 3.00 P M		C T	TF 6	6.3	Pony	0.0	62	D		Ar 2.50 P M
MON. WED. & FRI.	MON. WED. & FRI.								MON. WED. & FRI.	MON. WED. & FRI.

D—Day Telegraph Office.   W—Water.   C—Coal.   T—Table.   Y—Wye.

☞Study carefully Special and General Rules. Important changes have been made which must be understood alike by all.

Conductors will register at Sappington and Pony, and will not pass any registering station, which has telegraph service, without an order or clearance.

Trains must be under perfect control when approaching switches, also all bluffs where slides are liable to occur.

Switches at Sappington will be kept locked for N. P. & M. main track.

Passengers will be carried only on rear section of regular trains.

All car doors must be kept closed while in trains.

NORTHERN PACIFIC & MONTANA RAILROAD.—Second District.

West Bound. Mountain or 105th Meridian Time, One hour slower than Central or 90th Meridian Time. **East Bound.**

Built	MIXED No. 109 Sec'd Class Mon.Wed.&Fri.	BUTTE FREIGHT No. 59 Third Class DAILY	BUTTE PASSENGER No. 7 First Class DAILY	PACIFIC EXPRESS No. 3 First Class DAILY	Water, Coal Scales, Tables and Wyes	Station Numbers	Distance from Logan	STATIONS — Time Card No. 25 June 4th, 1893 Succeeding No. 24A	Distance from Butte	Capacity of Side Tracks	Telegraph Offices	ATLANTIC EXPRESS No. 4 First Class DAILY	BOZEMAN PASSENGER No. 8 First Class DAILY	BUTTE FREIGHT No. 60 Third Class DAILY	MIXED No. 110 Sec'd Class Mon.Wed.&Fri.
1889		De 1.35 AM	De 7.45 PM	De 11.20 AM	WCST	1120	0.0	Logan 5.5	70.7	150	N	See Page 2 / Ar 4.00 PM	See Page 2 / Ar 12.40 PM	See Page 2	
		2.00	F 7.56	F 11.29		TD 5	5.5	Three Forks 6.9	65.2	70	D	F 3.47	F 12.26	4.55	
		2.30	F 8.12	* 11.40		TD 13	12.4	Willow Creek 6.8	58.3	45		* 3.30	F 12.08 PM	4.30	See Page 6
	De 4.10 PM M60	3.00	8.30	11.52 AM M8	WCY	TD 19	19.2	Sappington 7.7	51.5	60	D	3.13	De 11.52 AM M3 / Ar 11.40	4.05	Ar 11.25 AM M109 / See 3
	4.45	3.35	F 8 48	* 12.05 PM		TD 27	26.9	Lime Spur 4.4	43.8	24		* 2.56	F 11.19	3.15	10.50
	5.05	3.55	F 8.58	* 12.13		TD 31	31.3	Jefferson Island 7.0	39.4	30		* 2.46 P60	F 11.05	De 2.51 / Ar 2.41 4P	10.30
6-14-90	5.45	Ar 4.30 / De 5.30	9.15	12.30	WCY	TD 38	38.3	Whitehall 7.0	32.4	100	D	2.30	10.45	De 1.45 / Ar 1.25	10.00
	6.15	6.10	9.35	* 12.48 M60		TD 45	45.1	Pipestone 5.9	25.6	28		* 2.13	10.23	De 12.48 M3 / Ar 12.43	9.25
	6.45	6.45	F 9.55	* 1.04		TD 50	51.0	Omsons Spur 2.7	19.7	10		* 1.57	F 10.05	12.15	8.57
	7.00	7.05	F 10.05	* 1.10		TD 54	53.7	Beef Straight 2.0	17.0	15		* 1.51	F 9.57	12.03 PM	8.45
	7.13	7.20	F 10.14	* 1.15		TD 55	55.7	Lumber Spur 3.4	15.0	6		* 1.46	F 9.50	11.53 AM	8.35
	7.30	7.45	F 10.25	* 1.23		TD 59	59.1	Lewis Spur 1.6	11.6	20		* 1.38	F 9.42	11.39	8.20
	7.45	7.55	F 10.30	* 1.28	W	TD 60	60.7	Homestake Tunnel 0.4	10.0	30	D	1.32	9.37	11.30	8.10
1889	7.50	Ar 8.00 / De 8.05 M110	F 10.32	1.30 M4		TD 61	61.1	Highview 7.2	9.6	28		* 1.30 M3	* 9.35	11.25	8.05 M59
						TD 68	68.3	East Butte 0.9	2.4						
	8.30	8.45	* 11.00	Ar 2.00 PM DAILY		TD 70	69.2	M. U. Transfer 1.5	1.5	100		De 12.40 PM DAILY	* 9.05	10.40	7.20
	Ar 8.40 PM	Ar 8.55 AM M8	Ar 11.05 PM		WCST	TD 71	70.7	Butte 0.0	0.0	300	N		De 9.00 AM M59	De 10.30 AM	De 7.15 AM
	Mon.Wed.&Fri.	DAILY	DAILY										DAILY	DAILY	Mon.Wed.&Fri.

M—Meet. P—Pass. *—Trains do not stop for passengers. F—Flag Station. W—Water. C—Coal. S—Scale. T—Table. Y—Wye. D—Day and N—Night and Day Telegraph Office.

Fullfaced figures (1, 2, 3, etc.,) denote meeting and passing stations.

☞ **Study Carefully Special and General Rules. Important changes have been made which must be understood alike by all.**

Conductors will register at Logan, Sappington, Whitehall and Butte, and must not pass any registering station, which has telegraph service, without an order or clearance. Nos. 3 and 4 will register at M. U. Transfer.

Trains must be under perfect control when approaching switches, also all bluffs where slides are liable to occur.

All trains and engines must reduce speed to ten (10) miles per hour over all truss bridges and high trestles.

Trains will not exceed schedule time descending mountain grades without a special order.

When handling air-brake cars, descending mountain grades, the retaining valves must be applied. Conductors will be held responsible for this duty as well as releasing valves at foot of grades.

When Nos. 3 and 4 meet at "Beef Straight," No. 4 will take siding.

On mountain grades brakemen must be stationed in their proper places, as per Rule No. 395, and in case of passenger trains ascending mountain grades, a brakeman must invariably be positioned on rear car.

All trains and engines **must come to a Full Stop** before passing over Montana Central Railway Crossing in Butte yard.

Switches at Logan will be kept locked for N. P. main track. Switches at Sappington will be kept locked for N. P. & M. main track.

No freights will be allowed to carry passengers.

All car doors must be closed while in trains.

J. D. FINN, Superintendent,
Livingston.

The Northern Pacific station at Helena, 1918.
Photo, Warren R. McGee.

The Northern Pacific-Union Pacific Depot at Butte, 1918.
Photo, Warren R. McGee.

LOCATION OF COMPANY BUILDINGS

Location	Dimensions	Construction	Date	Remarks
Muir		Wood frame	1883	Named after John Muir, contractor for first Bozeman tunnel (not the naturalist John Muir).
West End		Wood frame	1883	Constructed for tunnel operation.
Chestnut		Wood frame	1898	Connection to Turkey Trail Railroad.
Gordon		Wood frame	1883	Station served Fort Ellis.
Bozeman	24' x 120'	Wood frame	1883	Town's first passenger and freight depot.
Bozeman	30' x 92'	Brick	1891	Town's second station built for $15,000.

Bozeman	36' x 153'	Brick	1923	Major remodeling and expansion of second station.
Story (spelled "Storey" in NP Timetables)			1883	Confirmed stop.
Belgrade	Tower	Brick	1918	Built for operation of an interlocking plant for the lowline and highline. Operations building only.
Belgrade	20' x 100'	Wood frame	1886	Burned in early 1930s.
Belgrade	20' x 60'	Wood frame with stucco	1930	Replaced original depot.
Central Park			1883	Confirmed station.
Manhattan	20' x 60'	Wood frame	1884	Moved to Emigrant, Park County, in the mid 1980s, and used as a museum for a time.
Logan	24' x 54'	Wood frame	1890	Originally called Canyon House. Changed to Logan on November 26, 1889. Structure became freight depot.
Logan	30' x 100'	Wood frame	1891--1898	Placed on north side of tracks. Became major stopping point for all passenger trains.
Gallatin Station		Wood frame	1883	Located across the river from Gallatin City.

Trident	30′ x 74′	Reinforced concrete and wood frame with stucco	1911	This structure replaced a boxcar that was used for a depot.
Rekap				Only the foundation remains.
Clarkston				Formerly called Magpie.
Lombard	24′ x 120′	Wood frame	1891	Railhead of the Montana Railroad. Formerly called Painted Rock and Canyon Junction.
Three Forks	30′ x 40′	Wood frame	1890	Date is assumed.
Willow Creek	30′ x 50′	Wood frame		Similar to Three Forks Depot.
Sappington	24′ x 34′	Wood frame		Major cattle shipping point. Later became cross over for Milwaukee Road. Junction to the Red Bluff and Pony Branch Line.
Buell		Wood frame	1912	Waiting structure named for Buell Heeb.
Amsterdam		Wood frame	1912	Shipping point for agricultural goods.
Arnold		Wood frame	1912	Waiting structure named for George Arnold.
Anceney		Wood frame	1912	Major cattle shipping point. Named for Charles Anceney, Flying D Ranch.

CHAPTER THREE

MONTANA RAILROAD

The dream of money to be made from Montana silver and other minerals attracted Virginian Richard Austin Harlow to the notion of building a railroad that would connect smelter to mine. His proposed line would begin at Painted Rock on the Missouri River, in the extreme northwest corner of Gallatin County. Painted Rock was soon to be called Lombard after Harlow's chief engineer, A. G. Lombard. The 157-mile line followed the canyon of Sixteenmile Creek east to Maudlow, then northeast to Josephine, Sixteen, Leader (now called Ringling), Summit, Lennep, Martinsdale, Two Dot, Harlowton, then north, terminating at Lewistown.

Harlow intended to build a branch line to the then-thriving mining town of Castle in the hope he could transport silver ore from its mines to East Helena for smelting. The silver panic of 1893 forced him to change his plans for Castle, but he continued his intention to build the

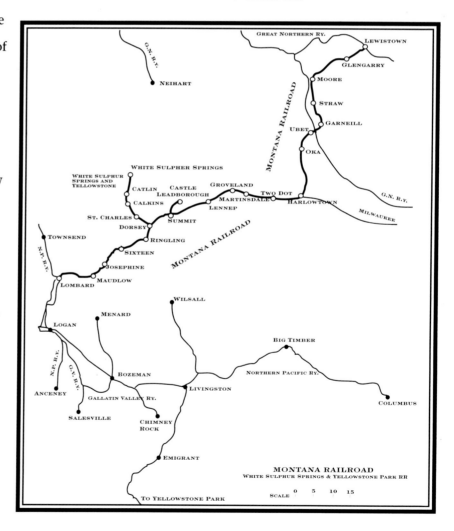

MONTANA RAILROAD
WHITE SULPHUR SPRINGS & YELLOWSTONE PARK RR

The beginning of the line for the Montana
Railroad, aka The Jawbone, 1904.
Photo, Warren R. McGee.

Near the Eagle Nest Tunnel Jawbone Railroad
close to the village of Sixteen, 1908.
Photo, Gallatin County Historical Society.

Upper right: A careworn depot at Ringling.

Below: The depot at Maudlow, 1922. Maudlow got its name from Maud Harlow, the wife of Jawbone founder Richard Harlow.

Photos, Gallatin County Historical Society.

railroad to Lewistown. With much persuasive talk and "jawboning," Harlow was able to capitalize The Montana Railroad in 1895. Montanans came to call the line "The Jawbone" after they experienced the railroad man's promises, with or without appropriate financial backing.

On shaky financial ground during most of Harlow's regime, The Jawbone was leased to the Milwaukee Road in 1910 after years of negotiation with Harlow. They paid him enough to relieve him of his debts, and he went back to Virginia. The Milwaukee made a series of changes, including moving the rails to run along the top of Sixteenmile Canyon, abandoning the tracks that Harlow had built along the creekbed. Heretofore, a trip on the Montana Railroad was an exhausting adventure. Passengers detrained at Lombard and often went to the hotel for recuperation. The Milwaukee re-outfitted the cars, making them more comfortable for travel. When the railroad finally acquired full ownership of the line in 1920, it advertised that it now owned a line that ran through some of the most spectacular scenery in the West.

The hotel at Lombard, 1910.
Photo, Warren R. McGee.

Top: The Milwaukee Railroad starts a bridge across the Missouri River at Lombard to connect with its main line to the west, 1907. The Northern Pacific Depot is foreground.
Photo, Gallatin Valley Historical Society.

Right: Watching bridge construction, 1907.
Photo, Gallatin Valley Historical Society.

Left: Publicity for the fledgling railroad town of Lombard.
Photo, Warren R. McGee.

Crossing the bridge at Lombard, 1910.
Photo, Warren R. McGee.

Montana Railroad Company TIME TABLE No. 19

Taking Effect at 12:01 A. M. Monday, June 3, 1907

For the government of employees only. The Company reserves the right to vary therefrom as circumstances may require.

EAST BOUND WEST BOUND

	FIRST CLASS No. 22 PASSENGER DAILY, EXCEPT SUNDAY	W- Water C - Cool Y - Wye	Station Number		TIME TABLE No. 19 JUNE 3, 1907 SUCCEEDING No. 18		Capacity of Sidings		FIRST CLASS No. 21 PASSENGER DAILY EXCEPT SUNDAY
LV.	9:30 A. M.	W.C.Y	0	0	LOMBARD N	157	63	Dispr. Agt.	4:00 P. M.
	9:57	W.	9	9	DEEP PARK	148	10		3:31 "
	10:12		14	14	MAUDLOW	143	20		3:15 "
F	10:24		18	18	JOSEPHINE	139	14		3:01 "
F	10:36		21	21	BAKERS SIDING	136	10		2:51 "
F	10:36		22	22	BAKERS	135			2:47 "
F	10:51		24	24	CANYON SPUR	133	8		2:23 "
F	11:01	W. 2.5 ml's east	27	27	SIXTEEN	130	11		2:09 "
F	11:28		36	36	MINDEN	121	14		1:44 "
	11:55 A. M.	C.Y.	45	45	DORSEY	112	14		1:19 "
	12:01 P. M.	W.	47	47	SPUR No. 47	110	10		
Arr. Dep.	12:11 " 12:31 "	Y. C.	49	49	SUMMIT	108	40	Dep. Arr.	12:59 12:39
	12:36 " mts. 21		50	50	LEADBORO JCT.	107			12:36 "
	12:46		52	52	DUBLIN	105	10		12:28 "
	1:08 "		60	60	LENNEP	97	14		12:04 P. M.
F	1:29 "	W. 1.5 ml's west	66	66	GROVELAND	91	7		11:45 A. M.
	1:41 "	Y.	70	70	MARTINSDALE	87	33		11:32 "
	2:11 "	W.	82	82	TWODOT	75	16		11:02 "
	2:48 " 1 mile east	C. Y.	95	95	HARLOWTON	62	50		10:25 "
F	3:17 "		107	107	OKA	50	10		9:55 "
	3:39 "	W. Y.	116	116	UBET	41			9:32 "
	3:53 "		121	121	GARNEILL	36	30		9:19 "
	4:12 "		128	128	STRAW	29	12		9:03 "
	4:38 "	W.	138	138	MOORE	19	30		8:37 "
F	5:03 "		148	148	GLENGARRY	9	12		8:12 "
Arr.	5:30 P. M.	W. C. Y.	157	157	LEWISTOWN	0	30		7:50 A. M.

SPECIAL RULES.

Trains will not exceed schedule time descending mountain grades. Engineers will exercise special care and caution...snow around sharp curves and bluffs. East-bound trains will not exceed ten miles per hour Leadboro Junction switch to Dublin. West-bound trains will not exceed ten miles per hour from Summit to Spur No. 47 and from Canyon Spirt Bridge and eight miles per hour Bridge 58 to Mile Post 22 West-bound freight trains will not exceed fifteen miles per hour from Dorsey to Lombard, without special order. Swith at Leadboro Juntion will be kept locked for main line.

Extra freight trains will not carry passengers except on special permission from the Superintendent. All employees of the Operating Department will be governed by the general rules of the Northern Pacific book of rules which may be had on application at office of Superintendent. All trains will run with the utmost caution and watchfulness wherever the new work is under way. No train having the right to the road must leave any station where it should meet a train until five minutes after its time and it must be observed at every succeding station until it shall have met the expected train. The five minutes are allowed for the variation of watches and must not be used by either train.

Number 21 has right over Number 22

F-- Trains stop on Flag or to leave passengers
* -- Trains do not stop.
N-- Night Office.

LOCATION OF MAIL CRANES

Maudlow, 8 telephone poles West of M.P. 14
Bakers,   22 "   "   "   "   "   20
Sixteen,   15 "   "   "   "   "   28
Lennep,   5 "   "   "   "   "   59
Oka,   - "   "   "   "   "   108

66

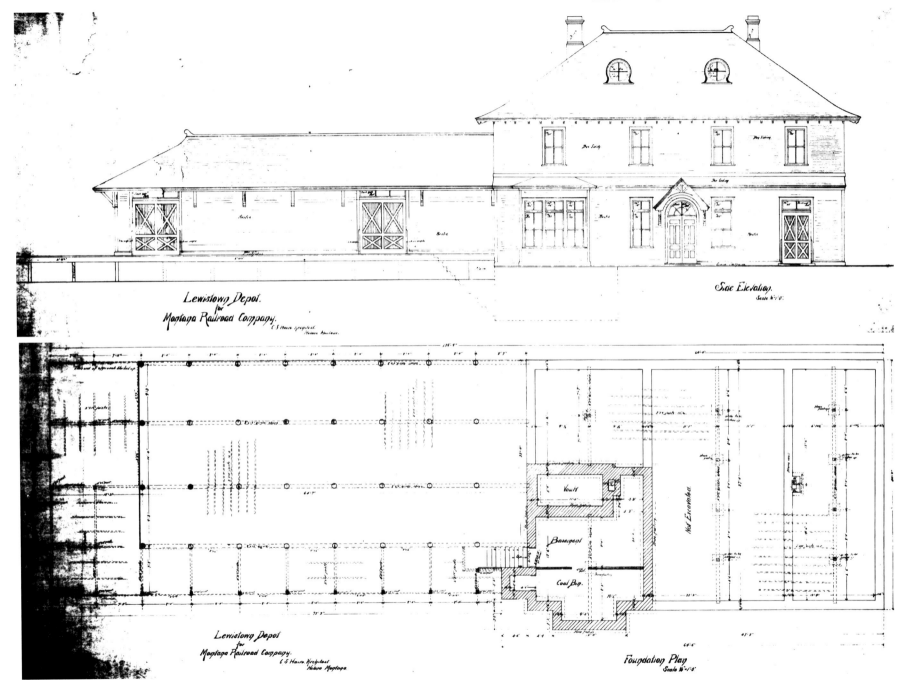

Lewistown Depot.
for
Montana Railroad Company.

Side Elevation.
Scale ¼"=1'0".

Lewistown Depot
for
Montana Railroad Company.

Foundation Plan
Scale ⅛"=1'0'.

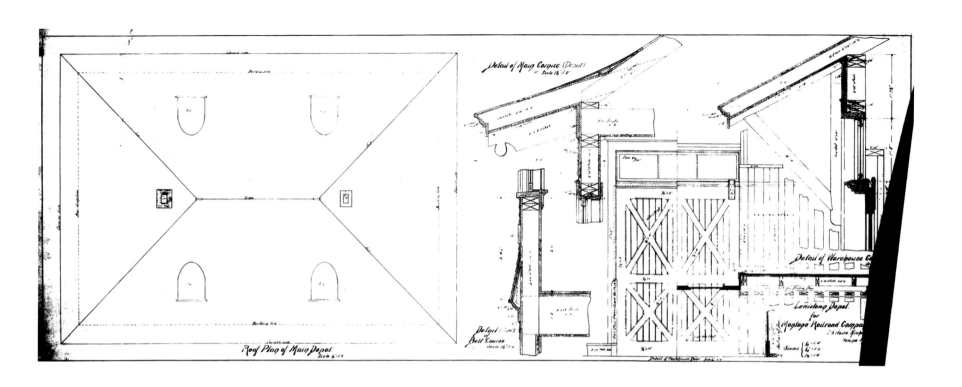

Roof Plan of Main Depot
Scale ⅛" = 1'-0"

Detail of Main Cornice (Depot)
Scale 1½" = 1'-0"

Detail of Warehouse Co

Detail
of
Belt Course
Scale 1½" = 1'-0"

Lewistown Depot.
for
Montana Railroad Company

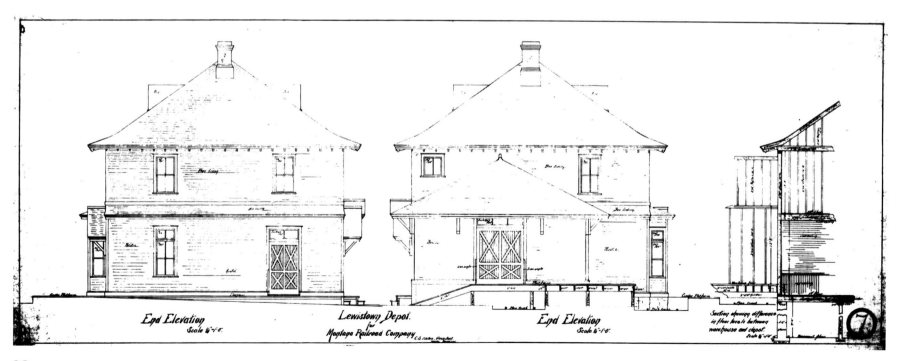

End Elevation
Scale ¼" = 1'-0"

Lewistown Depot.
for
Montana Railroad Company

End Elevation
Scale ¼" = 1'-0"

Section showing difference
in floor levels between
warehouse and depot.
Scale ¼" = 1'-0"

⑦

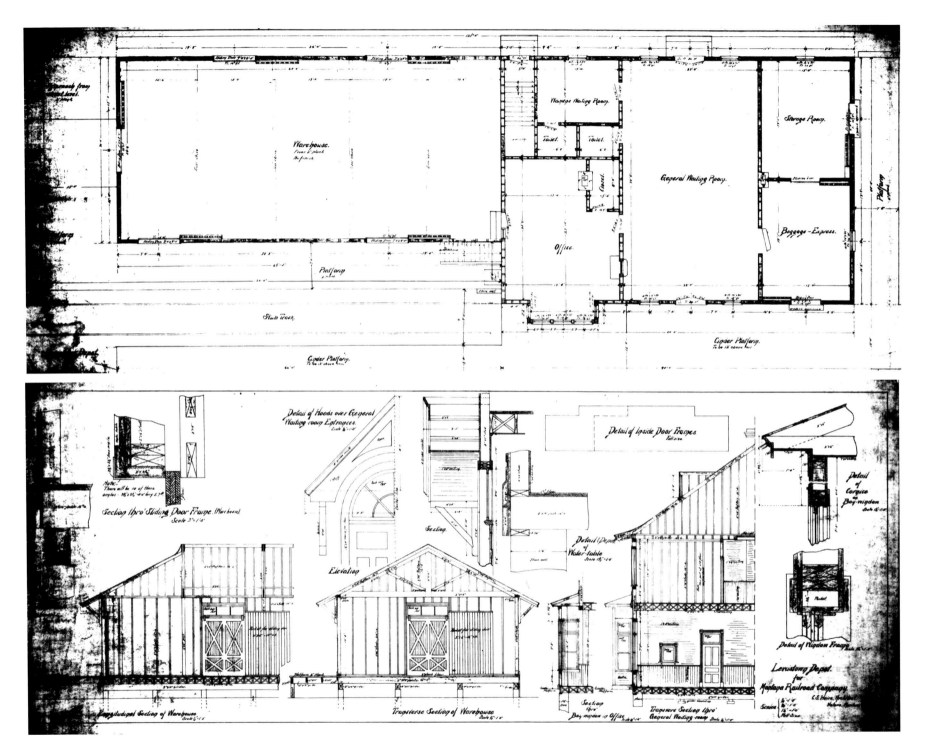

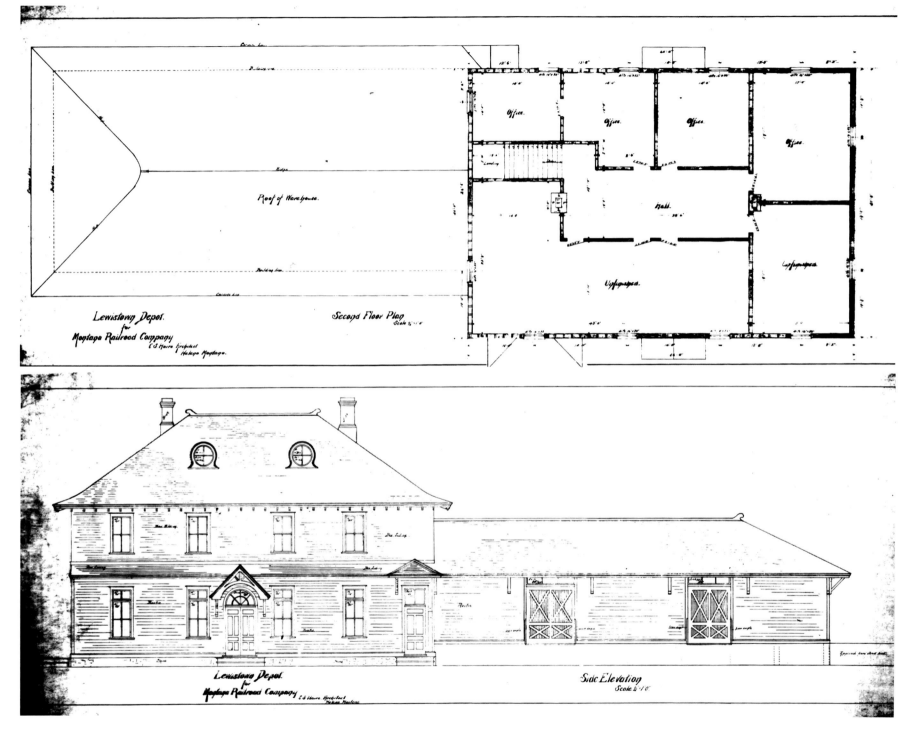

Lewistown Depot.
for
Montana Railroad Company
E S Moore Architect
Helena Montana

Second Floor Plan
Scale ½"-1' 0"

Office.

Office.

Office.

Office.

Unfinished.

Unfinished.

Hall.

Landing

Roof of Warehouse.

Lewistown Depot.
for
Montana Railroad Company
E S Moore Architect
Helena Montana

Side Elevation
Scale ½"-1' 0"

CHAPTER FOUR

CHICAGO, MILWAUKEE, ST. PAUL
AND PUGET SOUND RAILROAD

When the Chicago, Milwaukee, St. Paul and Puget Sound Railroad decided on a route through southern Montana on its transcontinental way to the Pacific Coast, rather than build new tracks and facilities, it bought up existing facilities. When the Milwaukee acquired the Jawbone Railroad, the company rebuilt the line along the top of Sixteenmile Canyon and electrified the railroad from Lombard to Harlowton. The Milwaukee also snapped up the Bozeman streetcar line and an interurban; both were electrified.

ACQUISITION OF BOZEMAN STREETCARS

By 1892, local Bozeman business interests had completed plans to construct a streetcar line using electric power generated by nearby Sourdough Creek. With considerable financial help from a group of Minnesota investors, they capitalized as the Gallatin Light, Power and Railway Company and did not plan to stop with a few city cars. Their dream was to build an interurban line serving the southern portion of the valley.

The *Bozeman Weekly Chronicle* reported on May 4, 1892, that "the Pray Lumber Company has commenced delivery of ties and planks. The erection of poles and overhead wire is under way." On June 29, the paper stated, "All grading has been completed and the ties have been laid. Rail laying has been started and residents should be able to ride by July 4." [13] Evidently, the newspaper waxed over-enthusiastic, as Independence Day came and went without the grand opening.

But on July 27, 1892, three little sparkling 40-horse power streetcars made their debut, leaving the Northern Pacific Depot to run through north Bozeman to Main Street and, eventually, up the hill to the college, a distance of two and one half miles. For the first run, local dignitaries had a free ride.

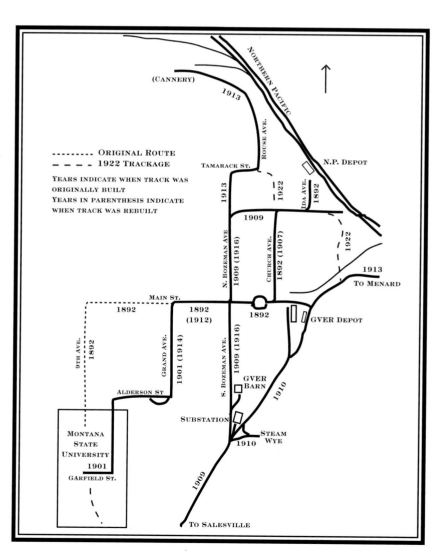

Below: Perhaps this is opening day, July 27, 1892, for the streetcar line in Bozeman. *Photo, Gallatin County Historical Society.*

Right: Official schedule for Bozeman's streetcar.

BOZEMAN STREET CAR SERVICE

--WEST-- EXCEPT SUNDAY --EAST--

Lv. DEPOT	Lv. HOTEL	Ar. COLLEGE	Lv.	Lv. HOTEL	Ar. DEPOT
				A. M. 7:50	A. M. 7:55
A. M. 8:00	A. M. 8:10	A. M. 8:25	A. M. 8:35	8:45	8:55
8:55	9:00	9:15		9:45	9:55
10:00	10:10	10:25	10:35	10:45	10:55
11:00	11:10	11:25	11:35	11:45	11:55
12:00	P.M. 12:10	P.M. 12:25	P.M. 12:35	P.M. 12:45	P.M. 12:55
P. M. 1:00	1:10	1:25	1:35	1:45	1:55
2:00	2:10	2:25	2:35	2:45	2:55
3:00	3:10	3:25	3:35	3:45	3:55
3:55	4:00	4:10	4:10	Ar. 4:20	4:25
4:25	4:30	4:40	4:40	Ar 4:50	4:55
4:55	5:00	5:10	5:10	Ar. 5:20	5:25

ALDERSON STREET

Lv. DEPOT	Lv. HOTEL	Ar. COLLEGE	Lv.	Lv. HOTEL	Ar. DEPOT
5:25	5:30	5:40	5:40	Ar. 5.50	......

A Special Car will meet Northern Pacific trains. Particular attention is directed to the cars leaving Hotel for College 4:00, 4:30, 5:00 and 5:30; and for the Northern Pacific Depot at 3:45, 4:20, 4:50 and 5:20 in the afternoon.

GET A BOOK OF TICKETS FROM THE CONDUCTOR--16 FOR 50C

The cars ran every day except Sunday; the schedule was arranged so that those desiring to board a Northern Pacific train could catch the streetcar and come into town, pass the Bozeman Hotel, continued on Church Avenue to the depot on Ida Avenue. Fare was ten cents during the day and twenty-five cents for a late night pick-up at the depot. In 1897, the Bozeman Street Railway Company took over management of the streetcar line and added another 1.28 miles of track.

When the Milwaukee Road acquired the line in 1910, the streetcars terminated their run at its new brick depot on the south side of East Main Street. Extra tracks were built to the fairgrounds but lasted a short time only due to lack of patronage. More track was added to the line in 1913, but by 1920, with auto ownership on the rise, the line was down to one streetcar. The Milwaukee people offered the City of Bozeman the streetcar business with a deal to throw in another car. The City of Bozeman turned their offer down. Late in 1921 the trolley line closed down for good.

A Bozeman streetcar departs from the Northern Pacific Depot before 1910, the year the Milwaukee Road acquired the line and built its own station. *Photo, Gallatin County Historical Society.*

Meanwhile, the dream of an interurban was taking shape. The Gallatin Valley Electric Railway was capitalized in 1908; ground was broken the following year. The electric line would run from Bozeman west to the Patterson Ranch, Ferris Hot Springs (now called Bozeman Hot Springs), Balmont, Chapman, Potter, Blackwood, Gilroy, Atkins, and on to Salesville (now called Gallatin Gateway). It would be the only interurban in Montana. At first, the line went only as far as Ferris Hot Springs; later the remaining track was laid to Salesville.

The Interurban car no. 10 at the Salesville Depot, 1909. Apollo "Paul" Busch is the conductor. *Photo, Bayard Todd.*

The Interurban and its passengers pose at the corner of Main Street and Bozeman Avenues, 1910. *Photo, Warren R. McGee.*

The Interurban rests beside the Milwaukee Road Depot in Bozeman, 1914. *Photo, Warren R. McGee.*

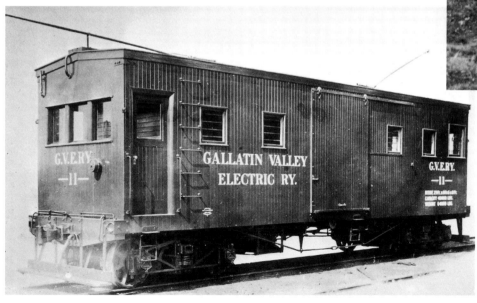

Box car 11 carried freight along the Gallatin Valley Electric Railway, 1910. *Photo, Warren R. McGee.*

Car No. 10, fifty-one feet long, made by the American Car Company of St. Louis, would accommodate seventy-five passengers, including twelve in the smoker. There were compartments for mail, express, and baggage. No. 10 featured a golden oak interior with rattan seats. Above the seats gleamed bronze baggage racks. The freight car, box motor No. 11, twenty-nine feet long, could carry twenty tons of freight. It soon carried barley and other agricultural produce to market. For the first time, high school and college students could live at home in the valley and make the daily run to school. Often accompanying them was their family's butter, cream, and eggs from the farm, destined for a Bozeman grocer.

In 1910, at the same time the Milwaukee Road acquired Bozeman's streetcar line, the company also took over the interurban. Officials announced that they immediately planned to build an ambitious electric line from Bozeman, Ferris Hot Springs, and on to Three Forks, joining its main line to the west.

The line carried both passengers and freight to the Hot Springs, then to West Gallatin, Holland, with a short branch line to Belgrade, then to stops at Camp Creek, Manhattan, Logan, and Carpenter, with the terminal at Three Forks.

The interior of the interurban car No. 10 featured brass fittings and rattan seats. *Photo, Ira Swett, "Montana Trolleys," Interurban Magazine, 1970.*

A new use for the Milwaukee Depot, Bozeman, 1932. The Gallatin Cooperative Creamery leases the station as engine #1265 pulls up with dairy products.
Photo, Gallatin County Historical Society.

At the same time, the Milwaukee announced it would also use steam engines to pull their heavier freight cars. On October 31, 1910, steam engines were rolling along electric train track from Bozeman to Three Forks. By 1914, the Milwaukee Road operated 16.36 miles of electric track and 34.31 of steam track in the Gallatin Valley, a small portion of their Montana holdings. At the end of 1930, all electric trains, including the interurban to Gallatin Gateway, were discontinued. The tracks were removed along the interurban bed; a portion of this bed in Bozeman, known as the Gallagator Park Trail, is a linear path used by walkers and joggers.

Bozeman's Milwaukee Depot
long abandoned, c1980.
William S. Hoy photo.

DEPOTS ON THE MAIN LINE

Plans for the Milwaukee Road stations can be classified into:

1) Designed Form

2) Standard Form

3) Modified Form

There are only two Designed Form Milwaukee stations in the Gallatin Valley; one is at Bozeman and the other at Gallatin Gateway. The majority look like those at stops all across the country — Standard Form. As with the Northern Pacific, the Milwaukee Road constructed depots from their own "System Standards" manual.

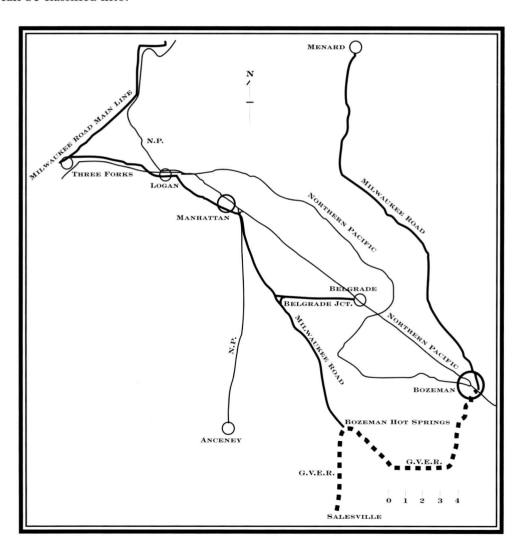

The Bozeman station was a Designed Form primarily because the Milwaukee Road was considering building a main line from Three Forks to Ringling via Bozeman. They also planned a direct line through Trail Creek to Yellowstone National Park but it never came to fruition. Thus, somewhat by miscalculation, Bozeman acquired a handsome brick station that also served as the depot for the Interurban. Down through the years, it has been used for a variety of purposes. It became a nursing station during the influenza epidemic of 1918. Years later, the building housed a dairy cooperative.

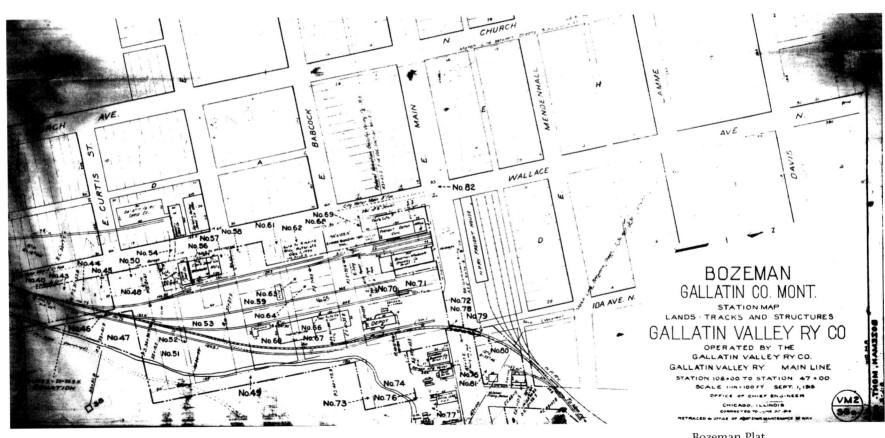

Bozeman Plat.

The elegant depot at Gallatin Gateway was the Milwaukee Road's way to lure tourists to Yellowstone Park. Milwaukee Road planners constructed a magnificent first class hotel where passengers could step off the train and move directly into the Gallatin Gateway Inn. Sightseers would spend their nights at the Inn, but take buses into the park during the day. Before the train rolled into the Gallatin Gateway station, however, Milwaukee Road passengers, according to *The Milwaukee Magazine* for June 1928, could "experience the pleasure of a sight of agricultural magnificence unrivaled in the West, as they glimpse through the car windows, the rolling Valley and broad acres of growing crops that evidence the fecundity of the soil; and see the splendid ranches and great dairy herds that graze over the rich pastures." The hotel itself was "built at a cost of a half million dollars by the Milwaukee Railroad, [and] is the handsomest and finest hotel in the State of Montana."[14]

The landscaping is yet to be completed at The Milwaukee Road's elegant Gallatin Gateway Inn, 1927. The nearby town of Salesville changed its name to Gallatin Gateway at about the same time. *Photo, Gallatin County Historical Society.*

Constructed in 1927, the Inn resembles a Renaissance revival. The building, though handsome, does not possess any regional characteristics. This station was the largest built in Gallatin County and by far the most elegant. Used primarily in the summer, the Gallatin Gateway Inn was built without insulation. It has since been refurbished for year-round use.

Tourists passed under this arch on their way to the west entrance of Yellowstone National Park.
Photo, Gallatin County Historical Society.

A typical Standard Form was used for the depots in Belgrade and in Manhattan. A two-story depot was constructed, each identical in plan and elevation. In both cases, the agent lived above the depot.

The station at Camp Creek was a smaller two-story Standard Form depot employing typical design features of the period, i.e., milled knee braces, horizontal siding with vertical base, wooden construction, little or no ornament, and a simple gabled roof. The Camp Creek Depot has since been moved to Manhattan and is now used as an apartment house.

Above: The Milwaukee's two-story depot in Belgrade is just finished. *Gallatin County Historical Society photo.*

Since mergers and buyouts of smaller railroads made up a major part of the Milwaukee Road's transcontinental route which passed through Gallatin County, those depots acquired from the Montana "Jawbone" Railroad were atypical and represented the Modified Form. The station at Lewistown was designed for the Jawbone by Helena architects Link and Haire. When the line did

Left: Camp Creek on the Milwaukee Railroad also supported a two-story depot. It has been since moved to Manhattan where it is used as an apartment house. *William S. Hoy photo.*

Above: The Milwaukee Road's #1919 passes the depot at Three Forks.
Photo, Gallatin County Historical Society.

Right: Winter at the Milwaukee's Three Forks Depot, c1980.
William S. Hoy photo.

The Milwaukee's "gate" to Yellowstone National Park at Three Forks, 1964. In the background is the Sacajawea Inn. *Olsen photo, Gallatin County Historical Society.*

For a number of years, the Milwaukee Road maintained its own hospital for employees, built at Three Forks in 1915. This building is currently used as apartments in Three Forks. *Photo, Gallatin County Historical Society.*

construct its own depots, it adopted a similar style for most of its stations with little concern for regional influences, not unlike the architectural plans for major retail and hotel chains across the United States today. A McDonald's or a Taco Bell look the same, wherever they are located. Outside the Gallatin Valley, however, the depots at Butte, Great Falls, and Missoula did not fit the mold; each had its individual flavor.

TURKEY RED SPECIAL

In 1913, the Milwaukee built a branch line from Bozeman curving north to Menard, the center of wheat country. The little train took its name from the kind of wheat grown in the area, which was stored at the Menard elevator. For one year or so, the Turkey Red provided daily passenger service as well as the hauling of freight, and all was bustle. Passenger service decreased to three times each week, then twice a week, then discontinued. Gradually, the trains went less and less to Menard, stopping for good in April 1978. The little depot became living quarters for a successive number of families. Then it was moved off the tracks one half mile away, acquired new siding, and is now a bunkhouse.

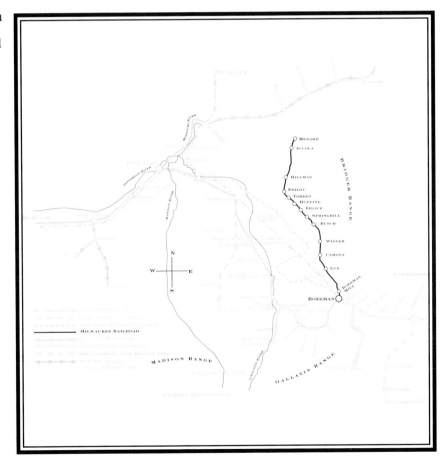

Above: The Menard Depot has outlived its original use. After the Turkey Red Special stopped its runs in 1978, a number of families lived in the aging station. A tractor is pulling the little depot to a ranch one half mile away. It is now used as a bunkhouse.
Photo, Gallatin County Historical Society.

Right: Milwaukee Road engine #461 pulls one of the last trains on the Turkey Red Special to Menard.
Photo, Gallatin County Historical Society.

Chicago, Milwaukee, St. Paul and Pacific Railroad Co.

ROCKY MOUNTAIN DIVISION

TIME TABLE No. 6

Taking effect at 12:01 A. M.
Mountain Standard Time

Saturday, December 1, 1945

For the government and information
of employes only

C. A. NUMMERDOR,
Assistant Superintendent.

N. A. MEYER,
Superintendent of Transportation.

J. L. BROWN,
General Superintendent of Transportation.

A. C. KOHLHASE,   **L. F. DONALD,**
Superintendent.   General Manager.

TABLE OF TRAIN SPEEDS

Seconds per Mile	Miles per Hour	Seconds per Mile	Miles per Hour
36	100	59	61
37.9	95	60	60
40	90	61	59
42.4	85	62	58.1
45	80	63	57.1
46	78.3	64	56.3
47	76.6	65	55.4
48	75	66	54.5
49	73.5	67	53.7
50	72	68	52.9
51	70.6	69	52.2
52	69.2	70	51.4
53	67.9	75	48
54	66.7	80	45
55	65.5	85	42.4
56	64.3	90	40
57	63.2	100	36
58	62.1	120	30

SECOND CLASS 263 Time Freight Daily	FIRST CLASS 15 Passenger Daily		Capacity in cars Sidings	Other tracks	Telegraph calls	Distance from Harlowton	Time Table No. 6 December 1, 1945 STATIONS	Distance from Three Forks	See Rule 6-A	Office open week days	FIRST CLASS 16 Passenger Daily		SECOND CLASS 264 Time Freight Daily
L 6.00 PM	L 6.59 AM			Yard	HY	0.0	HARLOWTON	114.2	BOEHJKO RTWXYZ	Continuous	As 11.47 PM		A 1.00 AM
6.15	7.08		68	11		6.2	VALENCIA	108.0	P	No Office	11.35		12.48
6.30	s 7.16		118	29	WO	12.0	TWO DOT	102.2	P	7.00 AM to 4.00 PM	11.28		12.38
7.00	s 7.33		119	17	MX	24.2	MARTINSDALE	90.0	P	7.30 AM to 4.30 PM	11.10		12.16
7.14	7.40		68	14		28.6	GROVELAND	85.6	PW	No Office	11.02		12.08 AM
7.35	7.50		110	25	UX	35.6	LENNEP	78.6	P	7.45 AM to 4.45 PM	10.54		11.55
7.57	7.59		69	10		41.2	BRUNO	73.0	P	No Office	10.43		11.38
8.15	8.09		119	51		45.4	LOWETH	68.8	PX	No Office	10.34		11.25
8.35	8.17		68	10		50.0	HAMEN	64.2	P	No Office	10.25		11.05
9.10	s 8.30		138	43	D	57.3	RINGLING	56.9	PV	Continuous	s 10.11		10.45
9.30	8.34		68	28		60.9	MOYNE	53.3	P	No Office	10.04		10.33
16 9.57	8.41		54			64.9	FANALULU	49.3	P	No Office	263 9.57		10.21
264 10.12	8.45		68	21		67.9	SIXTEEN	46.8	P	No Office	9.52		263 10.12
10.45	9.03		122	16		75.9	FRANCIS	38.8	P	No Office	9.34		9.47
11.00	9.10		36			79.8	NATHAN	34.4	P	No Office	9.27		9.36
11.08	9.15		108	17		81.9	MAUDLOW	32.3	P	No Office	9.23		9.29
11.30	9.26		71			87.6	DEER PARK	26.6	P	No Office	264 9.12		16 9.16 9.06
11.45	9.36		126			93.4	CARDINAL	20.8	P	No Office	8.59		8.35
12.10 AM	s 9.39			18	LD	94.9	LOMBARD	19.8	BPVX	8.00 AM to 4.00 PM 5.00 PM to 1.00 AM	s 8.56		8.25
12.25	9.44		68	12		98.0	BARRON	16.2	P	No Office	8.51		8.03
1.05	9.55		125	10		105.7	EUSTIS	8.5	P	No Office	8.41		7.48
1.30 AM	As 10.08 AM			Yard	FO	114.2	THREE FORKS	0.0	BEHJK BWXY	Continuous	L 8.31 PM		L 7.30 PM

EASTWARD TRAINS ARE SUPERIOR TO WESTWARD TRAINS OF THE SAME CLASS.

Automatic Block System is in use between Harlowton and Three Forks. Automatic Block System begins and ends at marker sign 30 feet east of east switch at Harlowton.

Mountain grade extends from west switch Bruno to east switch Loweth.

Sunday Hours

Harlowton ....Continuous
Martinsdale ....7:30 A. M. to 9:30 A. M.
Lennep ....7:45 A. M. to 4:45 P. M.
Ringling ....Continuous
Lombard ....8:00 A. M. to 4:00 P. M.-5:00 P. M. to 1:00 A. M.
Three Forks ....Continuous

Industrial Tracks Not Shown as Stations

Name	Location	Capacity
Higgins	3.7 miles west of Hamen	4 cars.

MAXIMUM SPEED PERMITTED PASSENGER TRAINS

Between

Harlowton and Lennep...65 miles per hour
Lennep and Bruno..40 miles per hour
Bruno and Loweth..35 miles per hour
Loweth and 3½ miles east of Ringling......................45 miles per hour
3½ miles east of Ringling and Moyne.......................65 miles per hour
Moyne and Fanalulu..40 miles per hour
Fanalulu and 1½ miles west of Sixteen....................65 miles per hour
1½ miles west and 4½ miles west of Sixteen............30 miles per hour
4½ miles west of Sixteen and Lombard.....................35 miles per hour
Lombard and Eustis...45 miles per hour
Eustis and Three Forks..65 miles per hour

MAXIMUM SPEED PERMITTED FREIGHT TRAINS

Between

Harlowton and Lennep...45 miles per hour
Lennep and Loweth..30 miles per hour
Loweth and Moyne...45 miles per hour
Moyne and Fanalulu..40 miles per hour
Fanalulu and 1½ miles west of Sixteen....................45 miles per hour
1½ miles west and 4½ miles west of Sixteen............30 miles per hour
4½ miles west of Sixteen and Lombard.....................35 miles per hour
Lombard and Three Forks..45 miles per hour

SECOND CLASS			Capacity in cars		Telegraph calls	Distance from Three Forks	Time Table No. 6 December 1, 1945 STATIONS	Distance from Bozeman	See Rule 6-A	Office open week days		SECOND CLASS
593												592
Freight			Sidings	Other tracks								Freight
Daily Except Sunday												Daily Except Saturday
L 2.00 AM				Yard	FO	0.0	THREE FORKS	38.4	BEHJK RWXY	Continuous		A 12.45 AM
							—4.4—					
f 2.15			18			4.4	CARPENTER	34.0		No Office		f 12.30
							—1.9—					
f 2.22			11			6.8	LOGAN	32.1		No Office		f 12.24
							—5.2—					
• 2.38			23	8	MN	11.5	MANHATTAN (N. P. Crossing) 0.8	26.9	P	8.00 AM to 5.00 PM		• 12.08 AM
							—4.8—					
f 2.51			23			16.6	CAMP CREEK	21.8	PW	No Office		f 11.36
							—0.9—					
f 2.54						17.5	BELGRADE JUNCTION	20.9	JY	No Office		11.25
							—2.9—					
f 3.03			24			20.4	HOLLAND	18.0		No Office		f 11.15
							—3.4—					
f 3.15			18			23.8	WEST GALLATIN	14.6		No Office		f 11.05
							—1.7—					
f 3.20			8			25.5	GREENWOOD	12.9		No Office		f 10.59
							—1.5—					
• 3.30			21			27.0	BOZEMAN HOT SPRINGS	11.4	JPY	No Office		f 10.50
							—2.5—					
f 3.38				9		29.5	BLACKWOOD	8.9		No Office		f 10.40
							—0.9—					
f 3.43			6			30.4	POTTER	8.0		No Office		f 10.35
							—1.7—					
f 3.49				6		32.1	BALMONT	6.3		No Office		f 10.25
							—1.0—					
f 3.52				9		33.1	MATTHEWS	5.3		No Office		f 10.20
							—1.6—					
f 3.58				6		34.7	PATTERSON	3.7		No Office		f 10.15
							—3.7—					
A 4.15 AM				Yard	BN	38.4	BOZEMAN	0.0	BOJKP RVWXYZ	7.00 AM to 4.00 PM		L 10.00 PM

Passenger trains must not exceed maximum speed of 45 miles per hour between Three Forks and Bozeman Hot Springs; other trains 30 miles per hour. All trains must not exceed maximum speed of 25 miles per hour between Bozeman Hot Springs and Bozeman and 15 miles per hour over Bridge CO-600, 1 mile west of Three Forks, and Bridge CO-654, ¼ mile west of Greenwood.

EASTWARD TRAINS ARE SUPERIOR TO WESTWARD TRAINS OF THE SAME CLASS.

WESTWARD							SIXTH SUBDIVISION					EASTWARD
			Capacity in cars		Telegraph calls	Distance from Belgrade Junction	Time Table No. 6 December 1, 1945 STATIONS	Distance from Belgrade	See Rule 6-A	Office open week days		
			Sidings	Other tracks								
		L				0.0	BELGRADE JUNCTION	5.2	JY	No Office	A	
							—5.2—					
		A	12	42	BG	5.2	BELGRADE	0.0	PR	8.00 AM to 5.00 PM	L	

Trains must not exceed maximum speed of 15 miles per hour.

EASTWARD TRAINS ARE SUPERIOR TO WESTWARD TRAINS OF THE SAME CLASS.

WESTWARD							SEVENTH SUBDIVISION					EASTWARD
			Capacity in cars		Telegraph calls	Distance from Bozeman Hot Springs	Time Table No. 6 December 1, 1945 STATIONS	Distance from Gallatin Gateway	See Rule 6-A	Office open week days		
			Sidings	Other tracks								
		L				0.0	BOZEMAN HOT SPRINGS	4.8	JPY	No Office	A	
							—2.5—					
				6		2.5	ATKINS	2.3		No Office		
							—2.3—					
		A	10	52	WA	4.8	GALLATIN GATEWAY	0.0	PRW	8.00 AM to 5.00 PM	L	

Passenger trains must not exceed maximum speed of 35 miles per hour; other trains 25 miles per hour.

EASTWARD TRAINS ARE SUPERIOR TO WESTWARD TRAINS OF THE SAME CLASS.

		Capacity in cars		Telegraph calls	Distance from Bozeman	Time Table No. 6 December 1, 1945 STATIONS	Distance from Menard	See Rule 6-A	Office open week days				
		Sidings	Other tracks										
	L		Yard	BN	0.0	**BOZEMAN** (N. P. Crossing 1.8)	24.7	BCJKPM RVWXYZ	7.00AM to 4.00PM	A			
						—5.5—							
		9			5.5	**LUX**	19.2		No Office				
						—1.9—							
		5			7.4	**CAMONA**	17.8		No Office				
						—2.6—							
		9			10.0	**BUSCH**	14.7		No Office				
						—2.2—							
			28		12.2	**SPRINGHILL**	12.5		No Office				
						—2.8—							
		5			15.0	**HUFFINE**	9.7		No Office				
						—2.7—							
		5			17.7	**EDILOU**	7.0		No Office				
						—1.9—							
		9			19.6	**HILLMAN**	5.1		No Office				
						—3.2—							
		9			22.8	**ACCOLA**	1.9		No Office				
						—1.9—							
	A		26		24.7	**MENARD**	0.0	Y	No Office	L			

Trains must not exceed maximum speed of 20 miles per hour.

EASTWARD TRAINS ARE SUPERIOR TO WESTWARD TRAINS OF THE SAME CLASS.

WESTWARD   **NINTH SUBDIVISION**   **EASTWARD**

		Capacity in cars		Telegraph calls	Distance from Bonner Junction	Time Table No. 6 December 1, 1945 STATIONS	Distance from Cottonwood	See Rule 6-A	Office open week days				
		Sidings	Other tracks										
	L		14		0.0	**BONNER JUNCTION**	40.0	JPYX	No Office	A			
						—1.3—							
		9	50		1.3	**BONNER**	38.7	BOPVWX	No Office				
						—10.9—							
			8		12.2	**McNAMARA**	27.8	P	No Office				
						—13.8—							
		47			26.0	**SUNSET**	14.0	W 5.7 Ml. East	No Office				
						—8.8—							
		16			34.8	**CLEARWATER**	5.2	P	No Office				
						—5.2—							
	A	20			40.0	**COTTONWOOD**	0.0	P	No Office	L			

Trains must not exceed maximum speed of 30 miles per hour, and when handling logs 20 miles per hour, and 15 miles per hour over bridge DD-302, ¾ miles east of Bonner.

EASTWARD TRAINS ARE SUPERIOR TO WESTWARD TRAINS OF THE SAME CLASS.

Nos. 592 and 593 will carry passengers.

At Three Forks, the normal position of the switch at the south leg of the wye is for the west leg and the normal position of the switches at the east and west legs of the wye is for the siding.

At Bozeman Hot Springs, the normal position of the switch at the east leg of the wye is for movement between Three Forks and Bozeman.

Rule 83(B) does not apply at Belgrade Junction, Belgrade, Bozeman Hot Springs and Gallatin Gateway when operators are not on duty.

INDUSTRIAL TRACKS NOT SHOWN AS STATIONS

Name	Location	Capacity
Miller Spur	5.7 miles west of Bonner	1 car.
Blanchard Creek	1.0 mile east of Clearwater	40 cars.
Chamberlain Creek	0.9 miles east of Cottonwood	Wye.
Sinton Spur	0.5 miles west of Manhattan	3 cars.
Goforth	4.5 miles east of Sunset	10 cars.

SUNDAY HOURS

Bozeman ....12:01 P. M. to 2:00 P. M.
Three Forks ....Continuous

The Milwaukee depot at Missoula, 1918.
Photo, Warren R. McGee.

LOCATION OF COMPANY BUILDINGS

Bozeman	26' by 95'	Brick	1911	Depot also used as Interurban Depot Freight house (1910), coaling plant, water tank, two-stall engine house (1912), two-stall electric car house (1906), sub-station (1906), stock yard, blacksmith shop, residence, outhouse, chicken house.
Patterson	8' by 8'	Wood frame	1910	Small lean-to used as depot, enclosed on three sides, open to the east.
Matthews	8' by 8'	Wood frame	1910	Lean-to and loading platform.

Balmont		Wood frame	1910	Lean-to and loading platform.
Chapman		Wood frame	1910	Lean-to and loading platform.
Potter		Wood frame	1910	Lean-to and loading platform.
Blackwood				Stock chute and yard.
Gilroy				Platform.
Bozeman Hot Springs		Brick	1910	Depot and power house, sub-station (1911), bunkhouse, shed, pump house, car house.
Salesville	20' by 60'	Wood frame	1910	Served as Milwaukee and Interurban Depot.
Gallatin Gateway		Wood frame	1910	Depot.
Gallatin Gateway		Wood frame with stucco	1927	Only station/hotel in the Gallatin Valley. Help quarters. stock yard, outhouse, coal & oil house, elevator, water tank, pump house, car department office & bunk house, ice house, battery charging building, coal dock (1927).
Belgrade Junction				
Camp Creek	20' by 30'	Wood frame	1911	Two-story depot with agent living above, moved to Manhattan for use as an apartment house.

Belgrade	24' by 80'	Wood frame	1911	Two-story depot with agent living above.
Manhattan		Wood frame	1911	Two-story depot, platform, stock yard, coal and oil house, outhouse, chicken house, loading platform.
Manhattan	24' by 70'	Wood frame	1950	Replaced old structure with one-story depot.
Logan		Wood frame	1910	Loading platform, small shelter for passengers.
Carpenter		Wood frame	1910	Loading platform, small shelter for passengers.
Three Forks	24' by 112'	Wood frame	1908	Had 150' pavilion north of the station. Structure remains near town.
Eustis	41' by 87'	Brick	1910	Sub-station for the electric mainline, no office.
Lombard	24' by 60'	Wood frame	1908	Passengers transferred here to Northern Pacific.
Deer Park		Wood frame	1897	Original station on Jawbone at tunnel.
Maudlow	24' by 80'	Wood frame	1897	Same as above.
Francis (Josephine)		Wood frame		Confirmed depot.
Ringling		Wood frame		Depot.

Dorsey		Wood frame		
Willow Creek		Wood frame	1908	
Sappington		Wood frame	1908	Crossing at grade of Northern Pacific.
Menard		Wood frame, one story, now used as bunkhouse	1913	Terminus of Turkey Red Special branch line from Bozeman.
Accola		Wood frame	1913	Small lean-to shelter on platform.
Hillman				
Edilou		Wood frame	1913	Small shelter on loading platform.
Torbet				
Huffine				Loading platform.
Erlice				
Springhill	8' by 8'	Wood frame, one story	1913	Depot, outhouse, loading platform.
Busch				Water tank, windmill, loading platform.
Wisner				Loading platform.
Camona				Loading platform.
Lux				Loading platform.

CHAPTER FIVE

UNION PACIFIC RAILROAD
OREGON SHORT LINE

West Yellowstone was still called "Riverside" when officials of the Union Pacific Railroad, realizing the growing tourist visits to Yellowstone National Park could spark new business, decided to build a branch line to the park's western entrance in 1908. The resulting Oregon Short Line served mainly as a passenger route between Salt Lake City and the park, by way of Idaho.

The magnificent stone and concrete depot, finished in 1909, was joined in 1922 by two compatible structures — a baggage building and an elegant dining lodge, designed by architect Gilbert Stanley Underwood. Trains were scheduled to arrive at the park boundary before breakfast was served at the lodge and to depart after dinner was finished. The lodge's Mammoth Room had a ceiling forty-five feet high and a walk-in fireplace. The depot itself had amenities not ordinarily seen in stations: wings which held dressing rooms for both men and women angled out from the main floor plans, each with a giant fireplace.

Although the Oregon Short Line could not operate during the winter months due to heavy drifting snow, the railroad continued to carry tourists east to the park until 1959. In 1980, Union Pacific donated the magnificent buildings to the town of West Yellowstone, which uses them for a museum, municipal offices, and art galleries. The roadbed for the Oregon Short Line is now used as a hiking trail.

UNION PACIFIC·

UNION PACIFIC DEPOT   WEST YELLOWSTONE, MONTANA

The elegant Union Pacific Depot at West Yellowstone. *Photo, Gallatin County Historical Society.*

Above: Detail at one of the entrances to the
West Yellowstone Depot.
Photo, Gallatin County Historical Society.

Bottom right: The Union Pacific's splendid
dining lodge at West Yellowstone.
Photo, Gallatin County Historical Society.

Union Pacific Dining Lodge - West Yellowstone, Mont 464

WHERE GUSH THE

GEYSERS

 UNION PACIFIC RAILROAD
OREGON SHORT LINE RAILROAD
THE NEW AND DIRECT ROUTE TO
YELLOWSTONE NATIONAL PARK

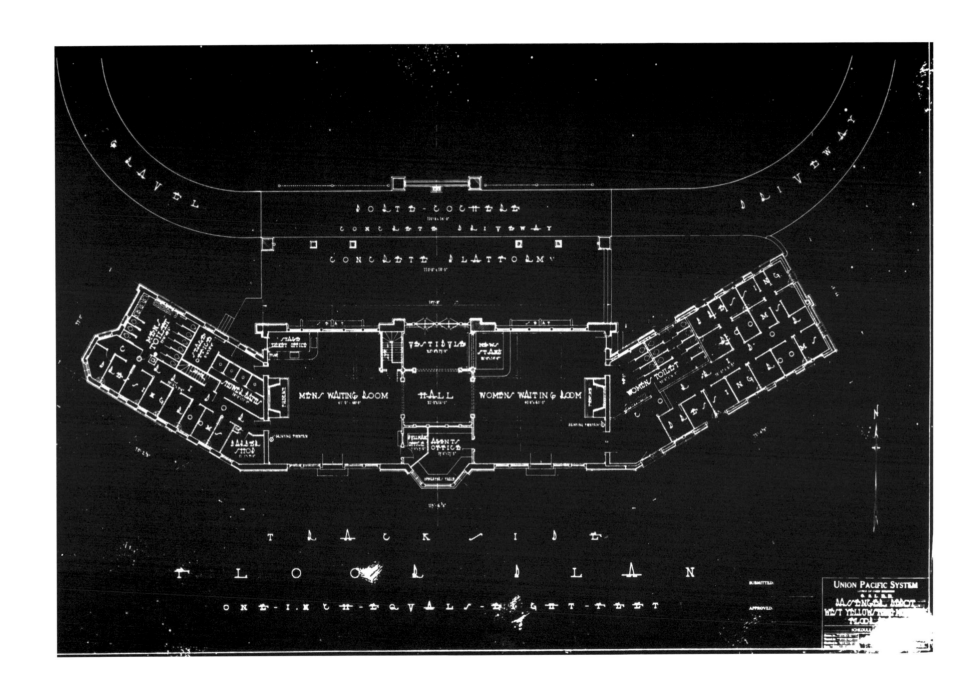

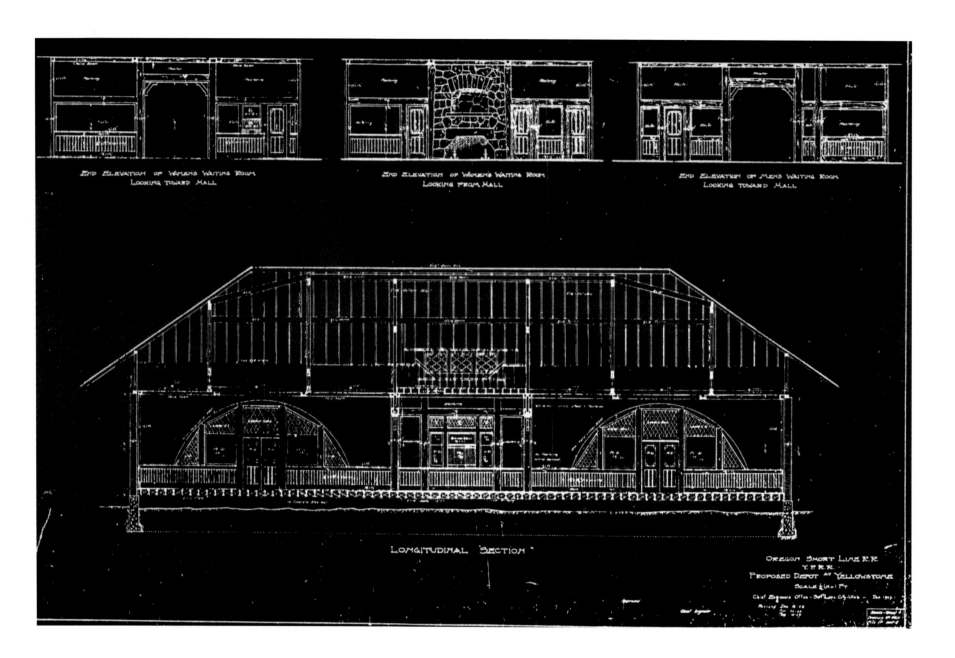

END ELEVATION OF WOMEN'S WAITING ROOM
LOOKING TOWARD HALL

END ELEVATION OF WOMEN'S WAITING ROOM
LOOKING FROM HALL

END ELEVATION OF MEN'S WAITING ROOM
LOOKING TOWARD HALL

LONGITUDINAL SECTION

OREGON SHORT LINE R.R.
Y.P.R.R.
PROPOSED DEPOT AT YELLOWSTONE

102

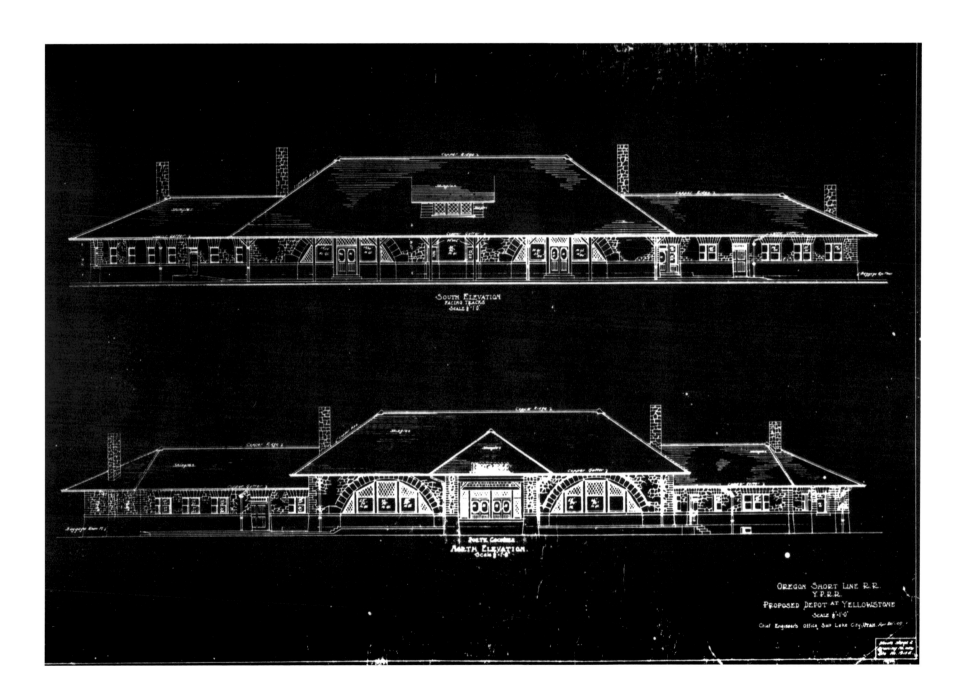

SOUTH ELEVATION
FACING TRACKS
SCALE

NORTH ELEVATION
SCALE

OREGON SHORT LINE R.R.
Y.P.R.R.
PROPOSED DEPOT AT YELLOWSTONE
SCALE
Chief Engineer's Office, Salt Lake City, Utah

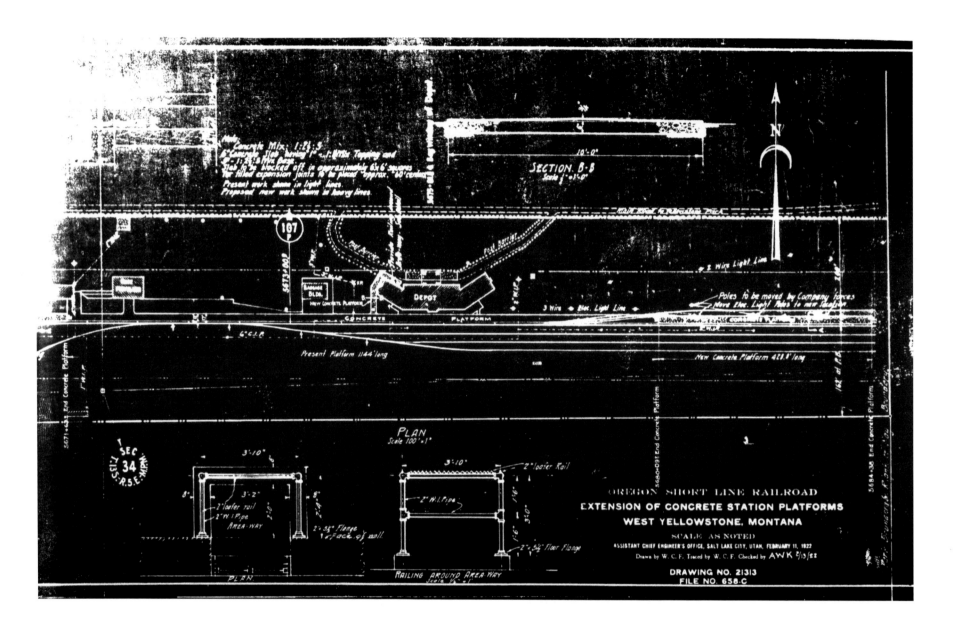

SECTION B-B
Scale 1"=1'-0"

OREGON SHORT LINE RAILROAD
EXTENSION OF CONCRETE STATION PLATFORMS
WEST YELLOWSTONE, MONTANA
SCALE AS NOTED
ASSISTANT CHIEF ENGINEER'S OFFICE, SALT LAKE CITY, UTAH, FEBRUARY 11, 1922
Drawn by W. C. F. Traced by W. C. F. Checked by AWK 2/13/22

DRAWING NO. 21313
FILE NO. 658-C

PLAN
Scale 100'=1"

PLAN

RAILING AROUND AREA-WAY

APPENDIX

The following are examples of plans taken from Book 2 of the Northern Pacific Standard Plans, c.1890.

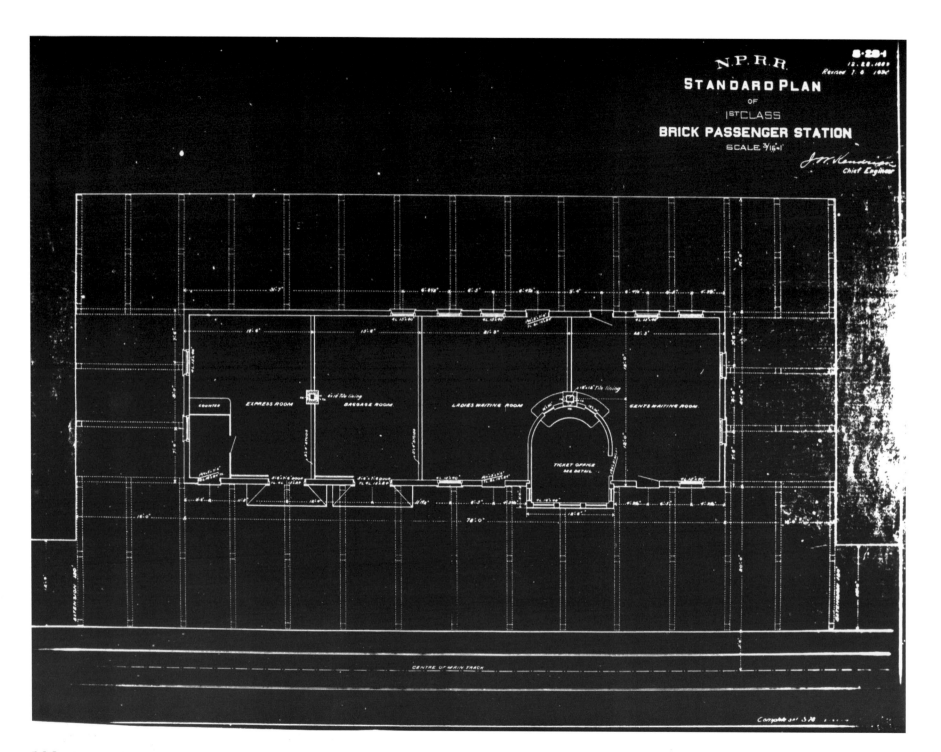

N.P.R.R.

STANDARD PLAN

OF

1ST CLASS

BRICK PASSENGER STATION

SCALE 3/16=1'

Chief Engineer

FRONT ELEVATION

END ELEVATION

FRAMING OF PARTITION BAGGAGE ROOM.

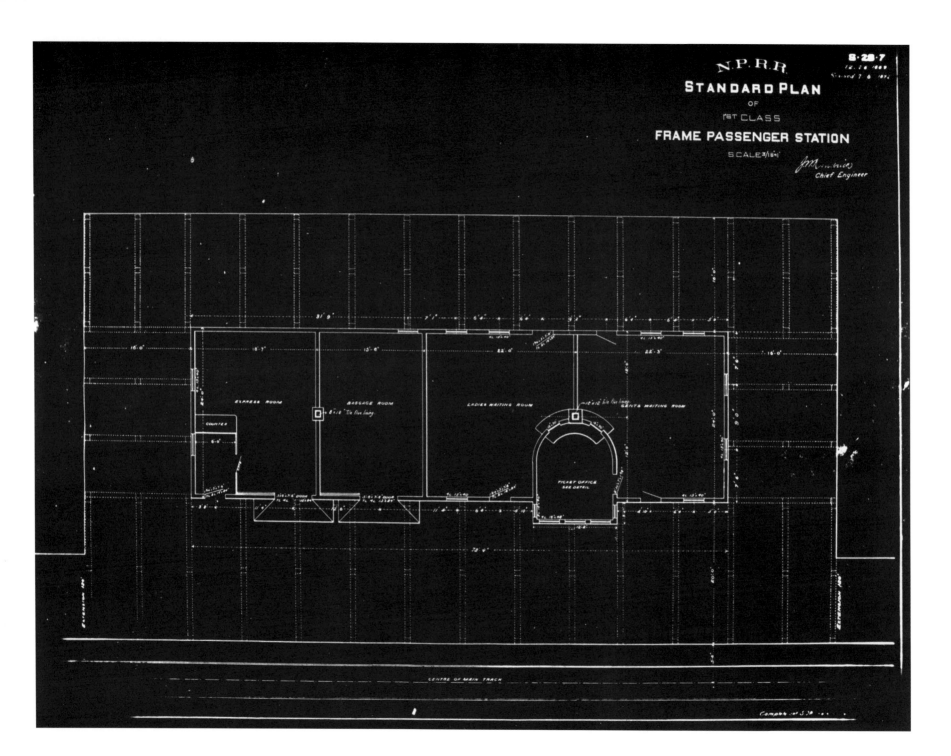

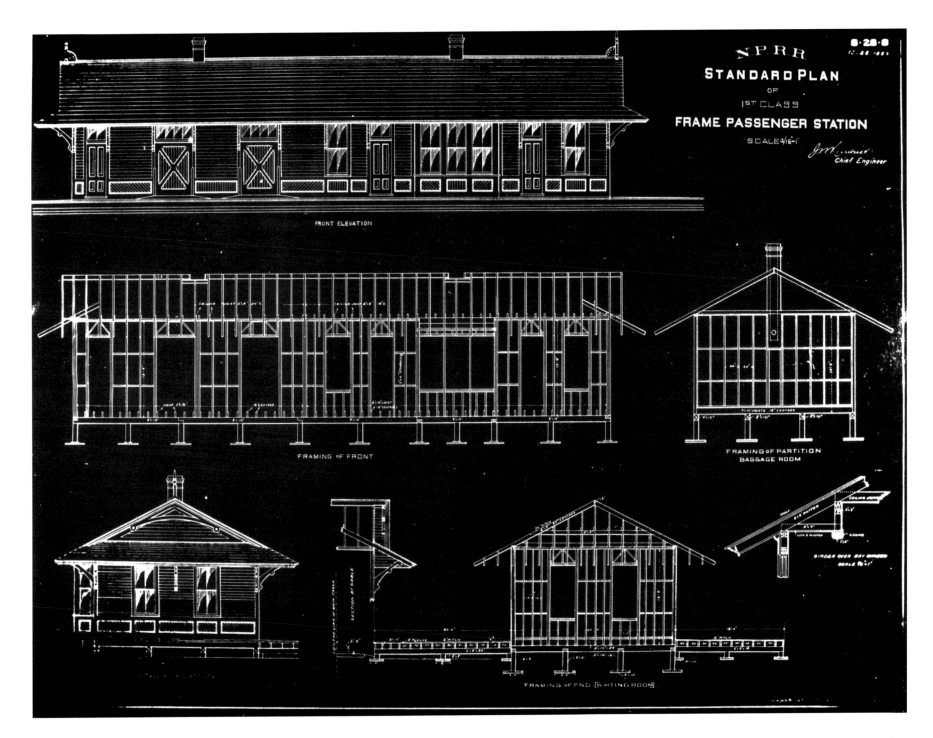

N.P.R.R.

STANDARD PLAN
OF
1ST CLASS
FRAME PASSENGER STATION
SCALE 3/16=1'

Chief Engineer

FRONT ELEVATION

FRAMING OF FRONT

FRAMING OF PARTITION
BAGGAGE ROOM

FRAMING OF END [WAITING ROOM]

GIRDER OVER BAY WINDOW

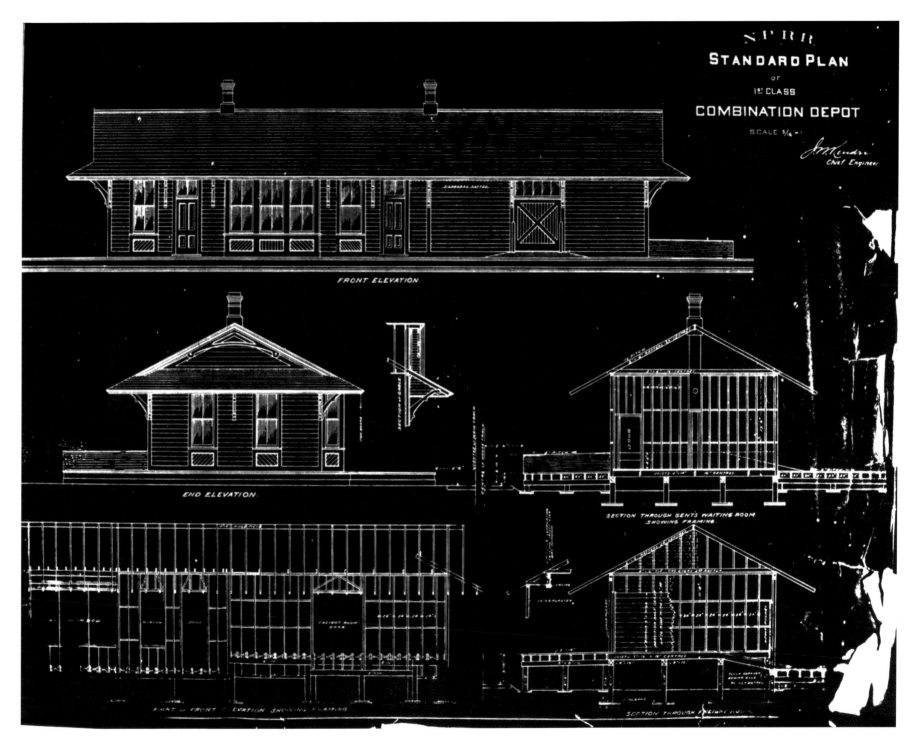

FRONT ELEVATION.

END ELEVATION.

SECTION THROUGH GENTS WAITING ROOM.
SHOWING FRAMING.

SECTION THROUGH FREIGHT ROOM.

N P R R
STANDARD PLAN
OF
1ST CLASS
COMBINATION DEPOT
SCALE 3/8 = 1

Chief Engineer.

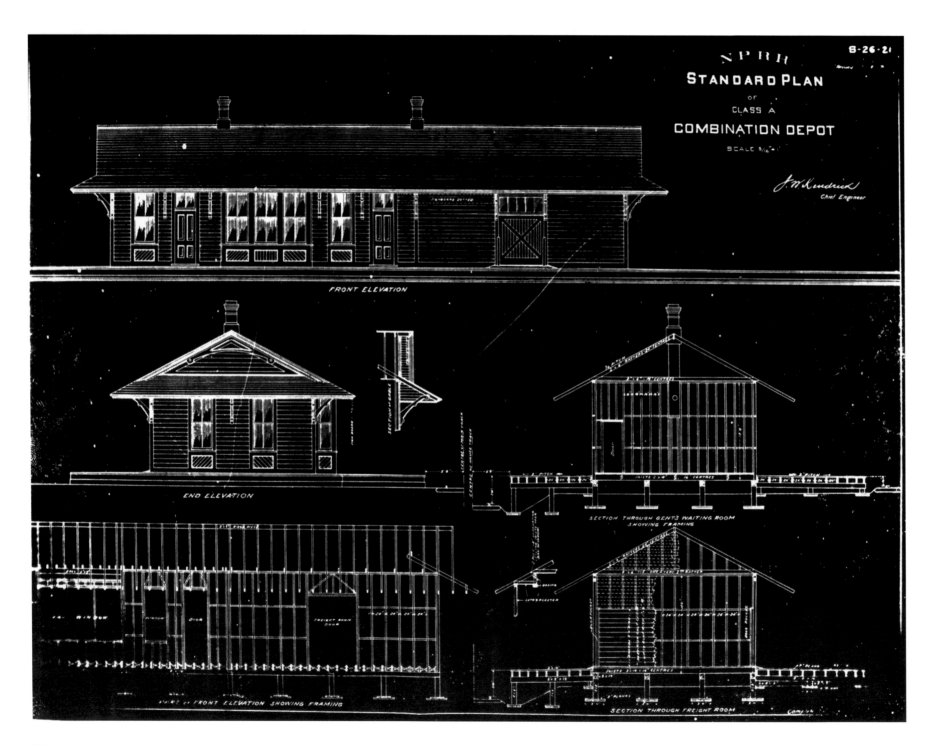

FRONT ELEVATION

END ELEVATION

SECTION THROUGH GENT'S WAITING ROOM
SHOWING FRAMING

PART OF FRONT ELEVATION SHOWING FRAMING

SECTION THROUGH FREIGHT ROOM

NPRR
STANDARD PLAN
OF
CLASS A
COMBINATION DEPOT

Chief Engineer

8-26-21

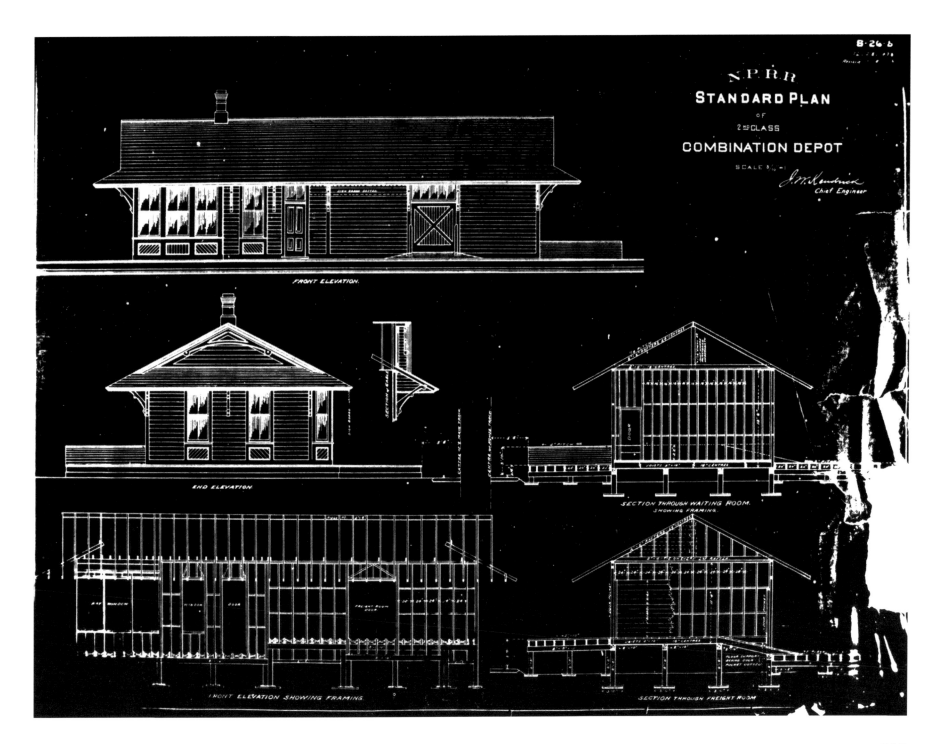

8-26-b

N.P.R.R
STANDARD PLAN
OF
2ND CLASS
COMBINATION DEPOT

SCALE

Chief Engineer

FRONT ELEVATION.

END ELEVATION.

SECTION THROUGH WAITING ROOM.
SHOWING FRAMING.

FRONT ELEVATION SHOWING FRAMING.

SECTION THROUGH FREIGHT ROOM.

113

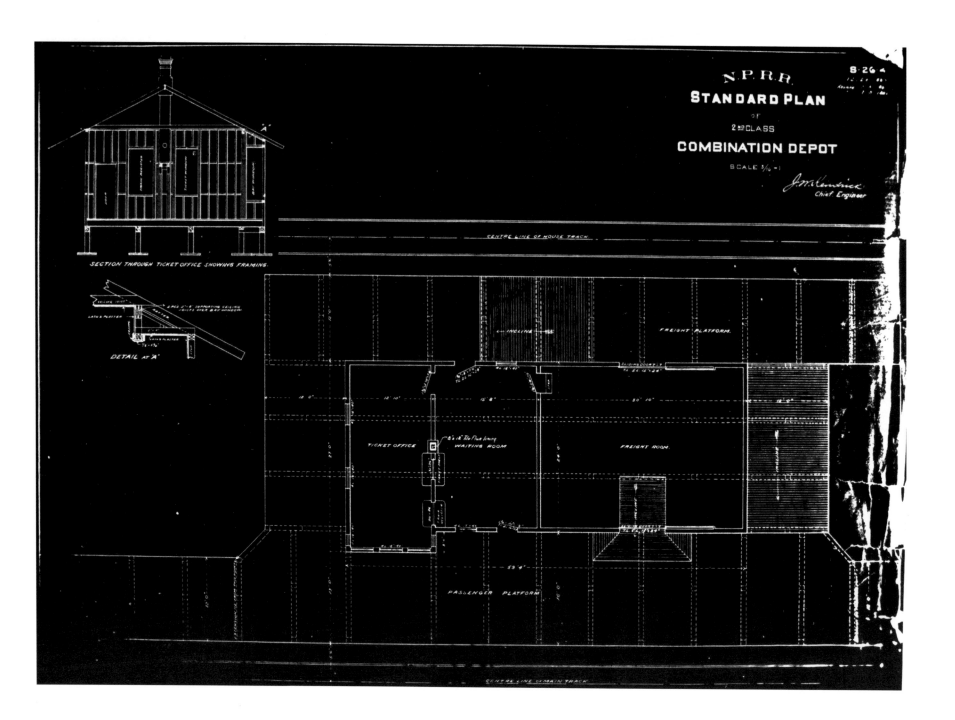

N.P.R.R.

STANDARD PLAN

OF

2ᴺᴰ CLASS

COMBINATION DEPOT

SCALE 3/16 = 1

Chief Engineer

SECTION THROUGH TICKET OFFICE SHOWING FRAMING.

DETAIL AT "A"

CENTRE LINE OF HOUSE TRACK

INCLINE

FREIGHT PLATFORM.

TICKET OFFICE

WAITING ROOM

FREIGHT ROOM.

PASSENGER PLATFORM

CENTRE LINE OF MAIN TRACK

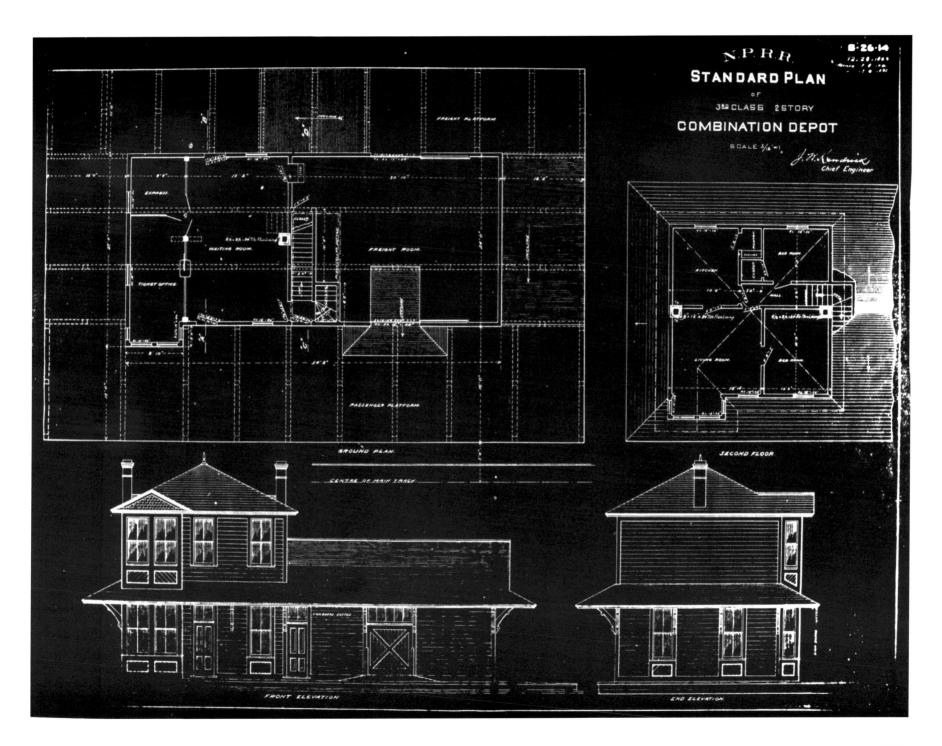

N.P.R.R.

STANDARD PLAN

of

3RD CLASS 2 STORY

COMBINATION DEPOT

SCALE 3/16=1

J. W. Kendrick
Chief Engineer

GROUND PLAN.

SECOND FLOOR.

FRONT ELEVATION.

END ELEVATION.

CENTRE OF MAIN TRACK.

115

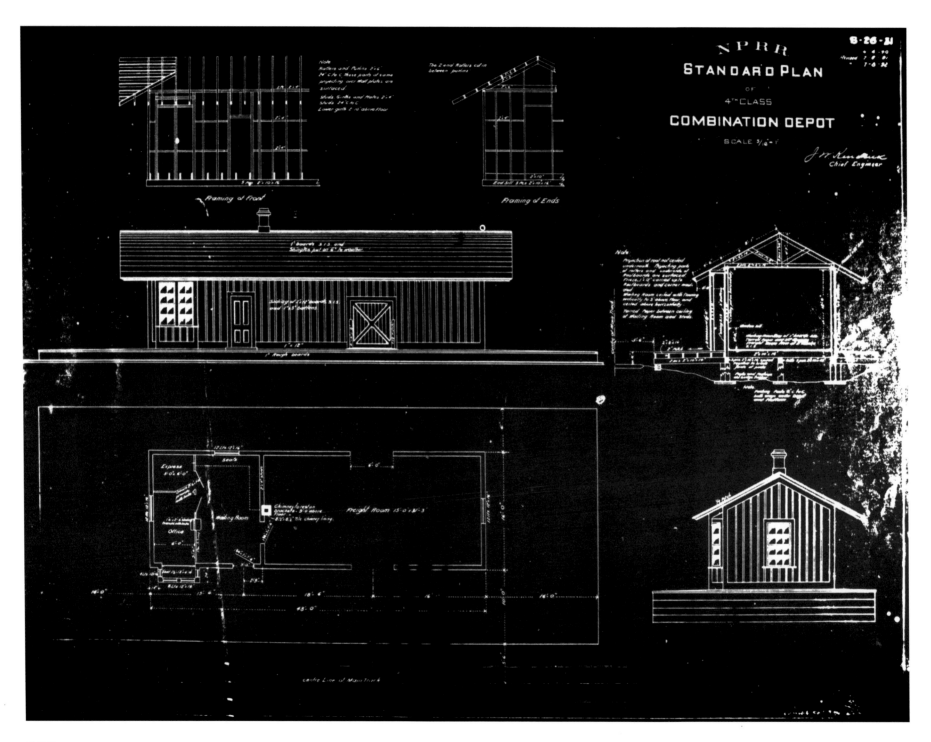

N.P.R.R.
STANDARD PLAN
OF
1ST CLASS ROUNDHOUSE

SCALE ¼=1'

Chief Engineer

FRONT ELEVATION

REAR ELEVATION.

SIDE ELEVATION

Complete Set S 32

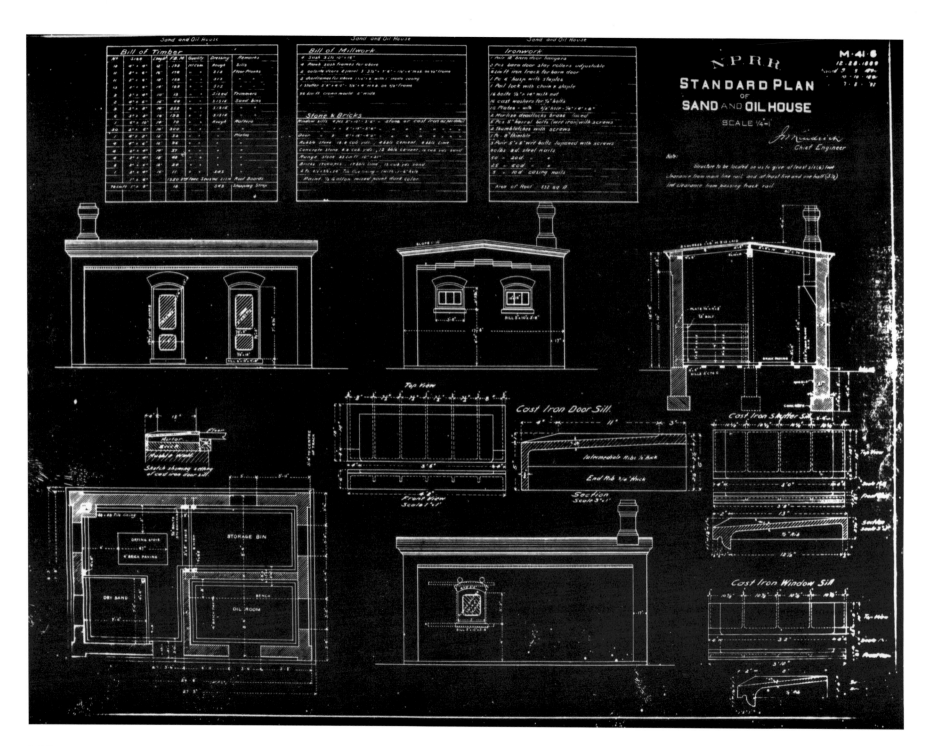

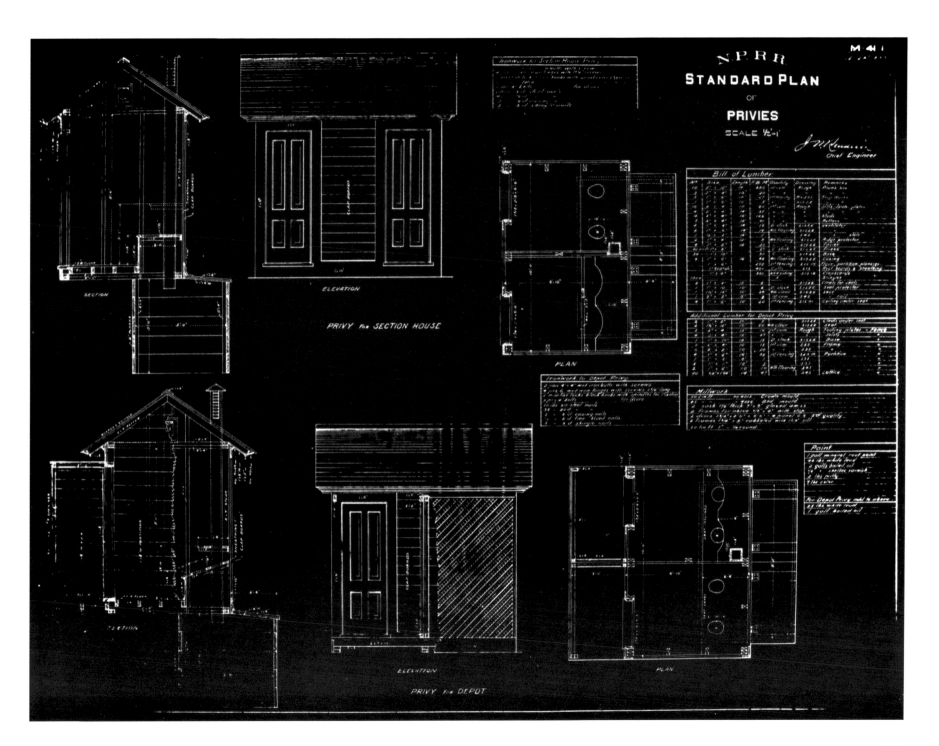

END NOTES

1. *Bozeman Avant Courier*, March 22, 1883.

2. Interview with Warren McGee, April 2, 1998.

3. *Bozeman Avant Courier*, July 4, 1891.

4. *Bozeman Avant Courier*, November 28, 1891.

5. *Bozeman Weekly Chronicle*, December 30, 1891.

6. *Bozeman Avant Courier*, April 21, 1886.

7. *Bozeman Avant Courier*, June 21, 1883, page 3, column 2.

8. Ibid.

9. Wheeler, Olin D. Wonderland, 1904. St. Paul: Northern Pacific Railway, 1904.

10. Ibid.

11. Ed L. Nowels, *Park County News, 1948 issue.*

12. Chet Huntley: *The Generous Years: Remembrances of a Frontier Boyhood.*
    New York: Random House, 1968, p. 155.

13. *Bozeman Weekly Chronicle*, May 4, 1892.

14. "The Gallatin Valley Line," *The Milwaukee Magazine*, v. 16 (June 1928) n. 3,p. 3.

SOURCES

Bates, Dorothy Chandler. Interviews regarding Manhattan Depot.

Bozeman Avant Courier, March 22, 1883, July 4, 1891, November 28, 1891.

Bozeman Weekly Chronicle, December 30, 1891, May 4, 1892.

Bozeman Daily Chronicle, December 21, 1947, August 9, 1964.

Burdett, R. M. and Janet L. Interviews regarding Logan Depot.

Burlingame, Merrill G. Interviews.

Chicago, Milwaukee, St. Paul and Pacific Railroad Company. Time tables from December 1, 1945.

Clark, R. Milton: "The Milwaukee's Gallatin Valley Line," *The Milwaukee Railroader*, v. 24, n. 2 (1994), pp. 4-14.

Fort Missoula Historical Society. Archives.

Fulker, Marguerite Pruitt. Interviews regarding Menard Depot.

Gallatin County Historical Society. Archives.

Green, Richard: *The Northern Pacific Railway of McGee and Nixon*. Seattle: Northwest Short Line, 1985.

In the Egypt of America, Gallatin Valley. Pamphlet. Bozeman: N. p., 1905 and 1908.

Lundwald, Les. Interviews regarding Manhattan Depot.

McDonald, Rita and Merrill G. Burlingame, "Montana's First Commercial Coal Mine,"
   Pacific Northwest Quarterly, v. 47, no. 1 (January 1956), pp. 23-28.

McCarter, Steve: *Guide to the Milwaukee Road in Montana*. Helena: Montana Historical Society Press, 1992.

McGee, Warren: Interviews.

McLeod, Gordon: Interviews regarding Norris and Harrison depots.

The Milwaukee Magazine, v. 16 (June 1928), pp. 3-6.

Montana Railroad Company. Time table #19, June 3, 1907 and October 8, 1908.

Montana State Historical Society. Archives.

Montana State University at Bozeman. Merrill G. Burlingame Special Collections.

Northern Pacific Railroad Company. Standard Plans, Book 2, c1890.

_____.Time Schedule, Montana Division, June 4, 1893.

O'Hern, Ethel. Interviews regarding Trident Depot.

Potter, Janet Greenstein: *Great American Railroad Stations*. Wiley and Sons, 1996.

Robertson, Donald B.: *Encyclopedia of Western Railroad History*, v. 2.
    Dallas: Taylor Publishing Company, 1991.

Swett, Ira, "Montana Trolleys III, *Interurban Magazine*, Winter 1970.

Todd, Bayard, Bozeman. Interviews.

Weigand, Melvin. Interviews regarding Logan Depot.

West Yellowstone Town Council. Archives.

Wheeler, Olin D. *Wonderland*. St. Paul: Northern Pacific Railway, 1895-1907.

INDEX